Me, Myself & Inc.

A Synergized World
An Energized Business
Living Your Ultimate Life

By Sherré DeMao

GreenCastle Publishing
137 Cross Center Road, Suite 239, Denver, NC 28037
www.greencastlepublishing.com
704.483.7283

Credits:
SPARK Publications, design and production
Gary Palmer, cover illustrations
Wendy Gill, editor
Wendy Allex, indexer

Library of Congress Control Number: 2009905965

ISBN 978-0-9841051-0-6

Printed in the United States of America

Dedicated to:

Pauline Williams Yantone Welch,
affectionately known as Granny Pea,
for her unwavering belief in me,
what I could accomplish, and
for inspiring the three promises.

My daughters Cassandra,
Amaria and Savannah,
who are my greatest source
of pride and influence in
creating a synergized world.

Table of Contents

Me
The family, friends,
community you.

Myself
The individual you.

Inc.
The business owner
professional you.

Introduction
A Synergized World ...
An Energized Business ...
Living Your Ultimate Life

As an entrepreneur with more than twenty-five years working with other entrepreneurs, I have found a common thread of dissatisfaction. It stems from all of us wanting the same level of passion and exhilaration in our personal life that we have for nurturing our businesses. Sometimes the entrepreneur gets to a certain level in business and yet wants more. Though much has been achieved, there is still this underlying sense that something is still missing.

Another scenario may be entrepreneurs who are not able to elevate their businesses to the levels they know are possible. Part of the dilemma lies in believing that personal goals should take precedence over business goals. Or perhaps in the ongoing tug of war between personal life and business life, nothing seems to be bringing the entrepreneur a real sense of satisfaction.

Noticing this common struggle, I began to take a closer look at the source of this discontent. In consulting with clients through my marketing firm, I insisted that they consider their personal goals alongside their business goals and incorporate them into their private "for their eyes only" business plan. The result? My clients made amazing discoveries. And even more exciting, these discoveries led to real action that made both business and life happen in a more satisfying and rewarding way for these entrepreneurs. From this point forward, I never did a business or marketing plan without personal goals being considered in the process.

The reality is that we tend to place ourselves in quandaries. We sabotage our ability to achieve our ultimate desires. In short, our lives are what our thoughts make it. Once we realize the power of our thoughts and perceptions, we are enlightened to the *probability* of achievement versus the *possibility* of achievement. We become enlightened to the power of goal synergy.

This book is written by an entrepreneur, with a focus on the entrepreneur. It is a culmination of what I have realized through practice and observation. In it, I share the experiences of real people who dared to synergize their goals in order to create the lives they wanted. I sincerely hope you will benefit as much from this book as I and others like me benefited from taking the journey ourselves.

"Once we realize the power of our thoughts and perceptions, we are enlightened to the *probability* of achievement versus the *possibility* of achievement. We become enlightened to the power of goal synergy."

Why Work/Life Synergy?

Work/Life Balance has become the mantra of executive coaches, training professionals, spiritual advisors, magazine articles and corporate values statements. Look in the dictionary and the definition for balance ranges from "a state of equilibrium or parity characterized by the cancellation of one set of forces by equal opposing forces" to "a satisfying arrangement or proportion of parts or elements." And herein lies the problem. We are viewing our personal and business lives as elements, parts and opposing forces. Everything is separate and in conflict, pulling and tugging as us from all directions.

This first section of Me, Myself & Inc. will help you re-program your mind to a better, more positive way of approaching your life and business — through Work/Life Synergy. Operating from a mindset of synergy versus balance immediately takes the guilt out of not being able to achieve balance. It takes all aspects of your life and business to a higher level because they are viewed holistically rather than separately. Therefore, what seemed unattainable before becomes suddenly attainable. Best of all, it is a pleasurable, energizing journey that will take you beyond what you could have possibly imagined.

"We as a society have had it all wrong. We have been focusing on the wrong side of the equation in this formula for a happier, more satisfying existence. It is not about balancing at all. It is something much greater and much more exciting and exhilarating."

Chapter 1
Stop Balancing – Start Synergizing

For many years of owning a business and living my life, I had been under the misguided notion that there needed to be balance. The problem was that it always meant choosing, adjusting, conceding, compromising, giving up and maneuvering this or that to achieve this ultimate equilibrium. I viewed everything being "balanced" as separate, competing forces vying for my attention and pulling me in all directions. As years continued to go by, I found myself getting more and more uncomfortable with the entire idea of balance. And I came to the realization that it is never achievable, at least not in the way that I or others perceived it to be.

Being the eternal optimist, I felt frustrated and disheartened by the idea that it was impossible to achieve balance. How could I accept this? How could I ever begin to bring everything into the needed order for me to have this elusive and ultimately desired balance? But then, I had an epiphany. We as a society have had it all wrong. We have been focusing on the wrong side of the equation in this formula for a happier, more satisfying existence.

It was at this moment of enlightenment that I began to change my entire view of how to achieve a satisfying work and personal life. It is not about balancing at all. It is about something much greater and much more exciting and exhilarating. It is about creating *synergy* in one's life.

Look up the word synergy in the dictionary and you will find definitions such as "the interaction of two or more forces so that their combined effect is greater than the sum of their individual effects" or "cooperative interaction that creates an enhanced combined effect." No conflict, no forces going against one another, but rather a true sense of harmony being achieved in the most desirable way — positively and energetically. And the best part of all? The combined effort enhances and enriches for an effect greater than those aspects separately could ever achieve. Now this is more like it! This is something I could embrace and run with ... and that is exactly what I have done.

MINISTER OF CHANGE

A CPA and Certified Financial Planner® considered himself to be a minister of change, continuously evolving to stay in step with the times and the demands of an ever-growing, volatile marketplace.

At the age of thirty-nine, after working for the corporate pleasures of others with much success, he determined to strike out on his own and start his own financial services firm. He had a wife and young children whom he wanted to spend more time with, and this desire inspired him to become, once again, a minister of change.

After being on the fast track, this accomplished professional determined that there was another road that leads to even greater wealth — the richness of a full and satisfying life. He resolved that his personal life was equally important as his work life, and from that day forward he set forth to blend his days to accommodate both. He began to view his time as yet another asset to be used wisely, getting up earlier in order to capture personal time to think, and then driving his children to school before heading to the office. On specific days, he blocked off lunch hours for working out at the local gym, which was within minutes of his office and home. He carefully planned blocks of time every week for in-person meetings at his uptown office and his suburban office. When he needed to be available for his family, he conducted teleconferences from his home office. He was able to attend his children's afternoon school events. And he conducted early morning financial analysis for his clients while his wife and children were still fast asleep.

He also made more time for himself by taking advantage of technology, creating systemized templates to use at various stages of his financial management and planning process. This brought his approach to the financial planning process out of his head and put it into a system that his employees could use. Consequently, they were of greater value and support to his firm, allowing him to focus on generating income and producing more time for his personal interests and family.

Talk to the successful financial services firm owner, and he will say that with synergy comes sanity. And with it comes the true measure of wealth … net worth not equal only to tangible investible assets, but coupled with a priceless treasure box of memories.

Several years ago, I started putting this concept into play when working with some of my entrepreneurial clients. I asked them to consider their personal goals along with their business goals when determining their short-term and long-term strategies. Understanding that many business owners feel forced to compartmentalize their personal lives and their business lives, I told them to accept and embrace the idea that these seemingly opposing forces could work together. I helped them accept this reality because as anyone who owns a business fully knows, their business is their livelihood and their lifestyle is reliant on their business and its success.

However, the caveat is that you must also accept that making a living is not the same as making a life. This was something I myself had to take a hard look at as I was making my life my business — until, of course, I was enlightened by the idea of synergy.

So, how do you create synergy in your life? First, you must take a very honest look at what you truly and ultimately believe will make you feel fulfilled, satisfied and complete in your personal life and in your work life. This is not as easy as it appears. Our entire mindset of opposing forces, conflicting needs and overwhelming demands has been conditioned into our thinking from a very young age. What gets your your heart pumping, your passion flowing, your energy soaring, your metabolism grooving, your mind racing and your future moving in the right direction? You *must* forget about all of those concerns tugging at your psyche and truly get to the very core of what you really, truly want. Only then can your journey towards synergy begin.

EXERCISE 1:1

Create a Goals Mind Map with two interlocking circles and spokes (as shown in the diagram below) on a large sheet of paper, such as an 11" x 17" ledger size or paper from a flip chart pad. Begin capturing your business and personal goals using the Goals Guide and Examples for reference, placing the items in the appropriate place on your Goals Mind Map:

- Goal
- Resources needed to achieve the goal
- Reasons for your goal
- Ultimate outcome once goal is reached
- Individuals affected by the goal

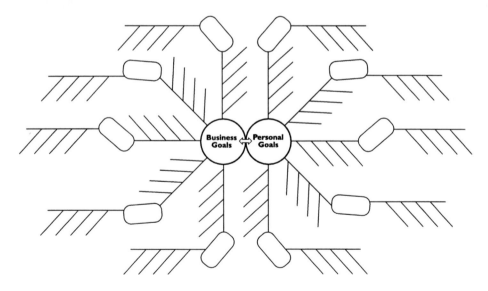

NOTE: You can also go to **www.MeMyselfandInc.com** and order downloadable templates to be printed on 11" x 17" paper or hard copies to be mailed to you.

Goals Guide and Examples

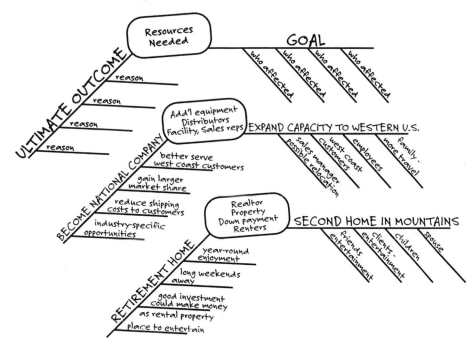

Write anything and everything that comes to mind, no matter how crazy, insignificant, dreamy, positive or negative it seems. Get it all down. Once you have done this, put your Mind Map down, walk away for a moment and then go back and look at it. Really look at it. Keep looking and adding ideas until you simply cannot think of another thing to add.

Most important is capturing *all* the reasons for your goals. This cannot be emphasized enough. If you are really being honest and disclosing all that you ultimately want or think that you want, and why, you will begin to see some things in a brand new way. You will begin to see for the first time where your mind's eye begins, your heart's desire beats and where other influences have made their marks in shifting your focus away from what you truly want to achieve.

Best of all, you will be looking at your goals — all your goals, personal and business — in one place as a whole. And this is where the process of true synergy begins.

"Everything in your life and business begins and ends with you. Accept that this is true and then realize that it is really about the mindset you operate from each and every day. If your thinking is holding you back, then it's time for a new way of thinking."

Chapter 2
Rewiring Your Thinking to Create Goal Synergy

Throughout my own journey, as well as in witnessing the transformation of others, I have found three key affirmations that seemed to resonate over and over again. These affirmations — or what I prefer to call promises — have become critical to the very core of helping me and others reach our goals. These same promises have been fundamental for succeeding over extensive odds. Now it is time to make these three promises to yourself — to help you synergize your life and work.

Promise #1: *I will either find a way or make a way.*

At first glance, this statement could be taken out of context and potentially do more harm than good, so let's get something straight right now. This promise is about determination and forging ahead toward your goals, but not doing so at the expense or detriment to anyone or anything. You must also make the agreement with yourself that at all times you will be impeccable in your actions and live up to your word.

In finding a way or making a way, it is about paying attention to opportunities, keeping your mind open to the possibilities and having the tenacity to not become discouraged in the face of disappointment, challenges and unexpected turns or delays. As a child growing up, I was blessed with the words of my grandmother, who said time and time again that I could do anything I set my mind to do. All I needed was faith in myself and my ideas. I reminded myself of these words countless times as I set out to go beyond my comfort zone in striving to achieve a goal.

When you set out to find a way or make a way, you are giving yourself permission to succeed. It's that simple. You are saying it is okay to be determined and to have this goal. You are saying that you believe in this goal and what it will bring to you and others as a result. With each goal that you apply this promise

From 80 to 8

The founder, CEO and president of a software training and support company for manufacturing facilities was ready to scale back her involvement in the company. She knew that she needed to groom some key personnel to step into leadership roles. In spite of her 80-hour workweeks, her goal was to continue to realize double-digit sales growth for her company, but take one workday off each week, plus weekends, to enjoy personal interests such as gardening and tennis. Her long-range goal was to be semi-retired — only going into work one day a week — and pursue new interests as well as domestic and international travel.

One key employee, a vice president in charge of operations, was a clear choice to step into the role of president for the company. Another IT engineer was an ideal prospect to step into a vice president role overseeing one particular division of the company. However, there were two challenges she perceived. The first was that the ideal V.P. candidate was living a state away and did not appear likely to want to relocate. The second was that there would be a need for a key support person, once the new president took over, to make the transition and operations run smoothly.

The first challenge was quickly dismissed when, to the owner's surprise, the V.P. candidate was more than willing to relocate with his family to oversee the division. The second obstacle was also quickly overcome. An ideal candidate for the support person position appeared unexpectedly — it was the newly appointed president's wife. It would have been easy for the owner to dismiss having a husband and wife working together to oversee the company as a bad idea, but she knew that the wife was extremely capable and organized. In all the times the couple had been in her presence, she witnessed a respect and camaraderie that put her at ease with trying the idea.

The owner saw her company flourish under the leadership of the president, his wife and the management team she put into place. Today the company continues to grow and prosper. The owner is realizing her ultimate life in semi-retirement, working only one day a week at best, enjoying without hesitation all the things she loves.

to, you can see its end result. You have such passion that it does not seem insurmountable.

Promise #2: *I will not feel guilty about making life easier for myself.*

This is probably the toughest one to follow. We as a society seem to like making things harder on ourselves as a required rite of passage toward earning a goal or achievement. Some of us think that if we don't do something entirely on our own, then we have not earned it purely or valiantly. Many of us have heard that you must work hard to be successful, and while this is true to a certain extent, we can stop working so hard at working hard.

What do I mean by this? Quite simply, as we work toward a goal, we need to take a step back every now and again and ask ourselves if there is an easier way to achieve the desired end result. Making a task or step in the process easier for ourselves is not slacking off or taking a shortcut, it's just plain smart. Why work harder when you can work more efficiently or receive help along the way?

We can also make life easier on ourselves by not taking so many things so personally and by not jumping to conclusions. How many times do we worry about things that never happen because we make assumptions about what *might* happen? During a setback, how many times do we undermine our own abilities to continue because we take whatever happened personally, instead of simply learning from the situation so it will be easier the next go around?

Once you make a conscious effort to ask yourself how a task can be accomplished more easily or how you can deal with your life more easily, you will be ready to adhere to Promise #3.

Promise #3: *I will keep my mind open to all possible support and resources.*

How open-minded are you…really? Sometimes people who perceive themselves to be open-minded (and demonstrate it at various levels) still hinder their abilities to reach their goals. That's because, once set on a certain path in their journeys, they discard possible options or are afraid to take risks.

What is most important to remember about Promise #3 is that you must be open to receiving support and resources from unexpected places. This is an area where people who have synergized their lives are strides ahead. They understand that a means of support or a valuable resource often comes out of nowhere. If you are not open to its potential, these can be easily missed. Sometimes this support or resource is right under your nose, but you have ignored or discarded it because of some obscure belief or perception that holds you back from seeing it as an opportunity.

Probably the most important aspect of adhering to Promise #3 is that by doing so, you are also following Promise #1 and Promise #2. You will be finding a way or making a way; plus, you will be making life easier for yourself in the process. Now doesn't this sound like a much more exciting way to move forward toward your goals?

As people put these three promises into action, they discover that they are in a better place to be at their best at all times. Being and doing your best is something that those of us who are goals-driven strive for on a daily basis. The reality is that sometimes we don't feel so hot. Then what? Well, at times when we are not at our best, having resources or support helps us to still *do* our best.

Everything in your life and business begins and ends with you. Accept that this is true, and then realize that it is really about the mindset you operate from each and every day. If your thinking is holding you back, then it's time for a new way of thinking.

EXERCISE 2:1

Now that you have had a chance to digest these three promises, take a moment to write them down and read them out loud. Write them every day until you can say them and feel them, making these promises your own. Make them such a part of your thinking that you keep each of these statements within your heart and mind each time you must determine your next step toward your goals.

Promise #1: I will find a way or make a way.

Promise #2: I will not feel guilty about making life easier for myself.

Promise #3: I will keep my mind open to all possible support and resources.

If you cannot keep a promise to yourself, then how can you possibly expect to realize what is yours to achieve? Everything in your life begins with you.

"The reason why balance is so impossible is that many of us are trying to balance aspects of our lives that aren't even a part of who we are or who we want to be. We are taking actions based on what someone else thinks we should be or wants us to be."

Chapter 3
Whose Goals Are They Anyway?

In the first chapter, we exposed all of our goals, both personal and work-related. Putting them all out there in our mind-mapping universe allowed us to see them as a whole, instead of as separate galaxies. We wrote them down. We recorded why we have them, no matter how silly or valid the reasons. We recorded what we expect from them, no matter how simple or grandiose the expectations. And we identified those individuals who might be affected if we reached them, as well as individuals or resources needed in order to reach them.

When I first took this new approach to analyzing my goals, I made another discovery. The reason why balance is so impossible is that many of us are trying to balance aspects of our lives that aren't even part of who we are or who we want to be. We are taking action based on what *someone else* thinks we should be or wants us to be. It is no wonder we feel conflict, opposing forces and other negative emotions. It is no wonder that as a result of this turmoil within, and without us even realizing it, we sabotage and impede our ability to have balance. Quite simply, subconsciously we are not sure these are aspects of our lives that we really want to balance. Therefore, we are not motivated to achieve goals that were never really ours anyway.

In this chapter, you are going to begin exploring the whole idea of who these goals really belong to. You will start to prioritize your goals and weed out those that are in the hearts of others, not your own. Through this process, you can completely and honestly analyze your goals. And by the time you have gone through the exercises, you will know whether they are: 1) your goals; 2) goals you think you should have; or 3) goals that have been imposed upon you by society, a loved one, or some other influencing faction. Then you can eliminate, without guilt, the goals that are not truly yours and focus entirely on those exciting goals that make you ready to take on the world. This is, by the way, making life easier on yourself.

Dot Calm

In 1997, when two brothers and a college roommate decided to start a website design and support business, they knew the hours would be long. They had to keep venture capitalists and investment bankers happy by demonstrating progress in the aggressive growth plan they had set forth. They also felt the pressure of living up to industry expectations of what a dot-com company should achieve in a certain period of time.

A short time later, the dot-com bubble burst, venture capital and investment banking commitments went by the wayside, and they were left to build a company on their own resources and tenacity to see it through in spite of the odds. Needless to say, this meant more hours than could possibly be imagined, as they set out to prove they could meet both the industry's expectations and their own. Within four years, they had achieved not only monetary success but market share success, and their business was named among the area's top website development companies.

At this point, the three of them were at a crossroads in their personal lives. All had young children, were in the midst of starting a family or were preparing to have children. The partners resolved from that point forward that there would be no more 80-hour work weeks; their families had to be as important as their business. They wanted to enjoy the fruits of their labor and participate in the joys and rewards of parenthood and supportive, loving relationships.

As a result, they established a less aggressive business growth plan and set the family values precedent across their entire company, with no-one working late. As one owner said, at 5:00 p.m. it reminds him of the Flintstones — the bell rings and everyone barrels out of the office, eager to get home to their families. Owners not only enjoy coaching leagues and taking extended weekends, they also enjoy the calm that comes with having life and work that energizes rather than drains.

In spite of the less aggressive growth plan, in its twelfth year in business, the company managed to double in size and sales, be a regional market leader, gain national market share and expand in capability through investment in other entities. Best of all, each owner can relish the true rewards of success, sharing it with those who matter the most.

The first goals that you need to analyze are those that appear to not be entirely yours alone. The reason I use the word "appear" is because you should not dismiss a goal as invalid just because someone wants you to achieve it. This could still be a very real goal for you. Someone else having that goal for you or along with you doesn't necessarily mean you can't embrace it. The key is to determine whether their involvement or desire is a catalyst or a roadblock, an inspiration or a deterrent, a confidence builder or a confidence buster.

Another issue to review involves answering the following questions: Which of *your* goals are *you* imposing on others? Which of your goals rely on someone else? Is the other person aware that your goal is dependent on him or her? Is this a goal you have identified for this person because it is necessary for you to reach your goal? Most critical, has the other person embraced this goal as his or her own, knowing that it is key to you reaching your goal — *or* are they reluctantly accepting the goal because of a sense of obligation, a desire for job security or a fear of disappointing you?

Those of us who are very goals-oriented naturally find ourselves with goals for others, both in our personal lives and at work. Also, because we are *so* goals-oriented, we tend to be somewhat intimidating to others. Without even realizing it, we may create in others a compulsion to please us or to advance in their jobs, resulting in an environment of guilt and dissatisfaction.

I have fallen into this category of being the goal imposer, even though I had quite effectively weeded out those goals that were not really mine. While I had already begun realizing a much more synergized existence (as a result of no longer being victim to others' expectations), I discovered I was potentially sabotaging my own efforts by imposing expectations on others. As the goal imposer, I had to come to terms with the reality that I needed to look for alternative ways to meet my own goals whenever the goal I imposed was not embraced by the other person. The best part is, once I did this, other goals that were much more synergistic in other areas complimentary to my own came to light. Open-mindedness and acceptance were absolutely critical to my being able to move forward into real action — for everyone concerned.

Against the Norm

When a young, ambitious forensic engineer decided to go out on his own, he was determined to be strategic from the very beginning. He had seen the pitfalls of other sole practitioner firms and vowed to steer clear of these mistakes. He did not just want to work for himself; he wanted to build a business that could operate beyond him.

His first move was to develop a company name that did not include his own name. Advisers cautioned against this move, but he knew that if his name was in the company name, it would be difficult to grow the company beyond him. In spite of a non-compete that forced him to take on work outside of a 150-mile radius, his reputation and work ethic resulted in substantial business as soon as he opened his doors. He was doing all the work himself, and within eight months he was overwhelmed, overworked and starting to fall behind.

Because customer relationships and quality of work meant everything to this engineer, he made a bold decision — to stop taking on new work for three months in order to hire the help needed to effectively serve his growing client base. He identified respected competitors, then notified clients he would not be taking on any new assignments for three months. He monitored the referred projects to make sure clients stayed happy and competitors were serving these clients as expected. In the meantime, he hired a bookkeeper, draftsman, administrative support, additional vendor support and a principal engineer.

Three months later, as promised, he announced he was ready to take on new assignments and the flood gates opened. In spite of advisers cautioning him that handing over work to competitors was the kiss of death, his clients continued with his firm in droves. They respected his approach and the fact that he had not left them hanging while in his infrastructure mode.

In his first phase of hiring and beyond, the owner always had the big picture in mind. The industry standard was to hire support for the owner practitioner. Typically, engineers were added to a firm to be a subset to the owner's expertise and talents. However, this entrepreneur-minded engineer saw things differently. He hired the expertise he did not possess so he could expand his company's base of knowledge and ability to serve. Without exception, every engineer on staff is older than him and has been in the business longer.

The owner also heeded some valuable advice from another entrepreneur to hire people who can take on responsibilities, not just manage tasks. By basing his hiring decisions on this mentality, he has continually evolved his firm to remain focused on the big picture.

In his fifth year of business, the owner continues to identify the next hires who will take the firm to an even higher level. This entrepreneur has realized a successful firm with a 70 percent growth in 2008 (in spite of a national economic downturn) and an average workweek of 45 hours versus 70＋ hours, plus he has the advantage of not having to think about his business every minute. He considers it an honor that his company helps support the families of his staff. When he does take time outside of work to think about his company, he focuses on business strategy and long-term sustainability, not on the day-to-day minutiae that occupies the thoughts of so many others in his industry.

By not heeding to the expectations of an industry and others who set previous standards of operation, he bucked the norm. This proved to be the secret to normalizing his business and his life — to the great satisfaction of all.

EXERCISE 3:1

Begin by looking at your goals that have an outcome that will directly impact or rely on someone else to achieve. You are now going to dig a little deeper to the core of the "why" and "what for" in regard to your goals. Make notes about the following three areas: happiness, pride and expectations.

The Happiness Trap: Will achieving this goal make you happier than you are right at this very moment? How and why will it make you happier?

Your ultimate happiness: If you did not achieve this goal, would you be unhappy with your life? Would not reaching this goal make it difficult for you to enjoy your life? Why?

Someone else's ultimate happiness: Does this goal hinge on making someone else in your life happy? If the goal is not achieved, will this person be unhappy with the outcome, or unhappy with you?

The Pride Trap: Will achieving this goal make you proud of the accomplishment for yourself and others? If so, how and in what way does this affect the outcome?

Your sense of pride: Are you doing it for you and you alone? Do you want this goal to prove something to yourself so that you can be proud that you achieved it against the odds? Why?

Someone else's sense of pride: Are you going for this goal to make someone else proud of you? Why is this important? Will you feel like you have let them down if you do not achieve it? Will you think that they will think less of you if you do not achieve it? Why?

The Expectation Trap: Do you feel an expectation to achieve this goal? Where did this expectation come from?

Your expectation: Is this an expectation you determined on your own? If so, is it one you consider a desired challenge or is it something you just want to achieve so you can move on to something else?

Someone else's expectation for you: Was this expectation imposed upon you by someone else? Do you now feel obligated because you do not want to let this person down? Why?

Valid or Invalid: Based on your assessment of happiness, pride and expectations, is this goal a valid goal for you? Is it truly desired by you to be more satisfied with your life? Hopefully, as a result of this exercise, you will begin to see which goals are truly yours and which goals are ultimately someone else's that you simply adopted out of a sense of obligation, pride, or to make others happy.

EXERCISE 3:2

Now that you have assessed all your goals that involve other people, can you eliminate some of these goals or re-evaluate them to make them your own? Chances are that this is getting a bit uncomfortable, because eliminating these goals will in turn affect others in the process. But remember, don't feel guilty about making life easier on yourself. And don't be afraid to be honest with yourself and others by simply saying a particular goal is not one you have a passion for. Those who really matter in your life will support you. Those who don't and try to make you feel guilty are not the type of people you need in your life anyway. I know, because as a result of coming to these realizations, I made significant changes in my life to eliminate all those "others" who were draining me emotionally and affecting my ability to focus on what would help me synergize my life, including clients, vendors and fair weather friends. You can do the same.

"The problem with the balance mindset is that it is continuously focusing on what is out of balance. We are reacting versus being proactive in our attempts to achieve this elusive idea of balance."

Chapter 4
The Balancing Act

We live in a society that has conditioned us to believe that we should leave our work at the office and our personal lives at home. On the surface, and for clear proprietary reasons, this makes logical sense and seems like sound advice, but we have taken this idea to the extreme — and to the point of dysfunction. Now, in our efforts to reverse this trend, we have created immense pressure to create balance between our personal and work lives. For the longest time, we were told we must keep them entirely separate to be happy. Companies would not allow fraternizing among employees at certain levels or allow married couples to work in the same place. Some companies still have these policies in place.

When the idea of keeping the two worlds separate was in vogue, those who attempted to create harmony between their work and personal lives felt like they had to split themselves in half. A feeling of wholeness seemed unachievable as our personal and work lives were compartmentalized by design and expectation. Our two worlds were competing for our attention — neither one fed and nurtured the other for success.

For the entrepreneur, keeping work and life separate is near to impossible. Therefore, living up to what society has dictated creates and adds pressure to the entrepreneur for a variety of reasons. Owning your own business becomes a double-edged sword. On one side is the fantasy of the American dream ... and on the other side is the harsh reality of building something from nothing, all on your own.

There is a misperception that entrepreneurs enjoy great flexibility. Those looking at you and your business from the outside envy your ability to set your own schedule, do as you please, arrive and leave work when you want and have no one to answer to but yourself. I know that you are snickering right now and saying, "Yeah right! I have customers and employees to answer to. I have a payroll to meet and deadlines looming. I would love to come and go whenever I please, but it seems I am coming

TGIF

The owner of a soil testing and construction monitoring firm was in the midst of a major expansion. He was about to launch an innovative division, requiring more resources in technology, people, capital and time. In a planning and strategy session, which included more than half of his 20+ person team, the strategic consultant shifted gears a bit and asked each team member what some of their personal goals were outside of work. A hush came over the room as this had never been explored before.

One employee shared without pause a concern: "What if someone's personal goals are in direct conflict with their work goals? Will this affect their position with the company?" Of course, this was exactly why the question was being posed — to help everyone know one another a bit better, as well as to open the owner's eyes about each team member's life outside of his company. The purpose of this exercise was to keep the team's passion alive, since many of these workers had joined the firm when it was just a handful of people. Job demands had increased and all were feeling the challenge of "balancing" work and life.

Part of keeping them passionate was also showing respect and acknowledging who they were as individuals outside of work. As workers shared their personal goals, one by one, a common thread became evident. A longer weekend or some personal time during the week would allow workers to pursue their interests, which ranged from a rock band to gardening to caring for an elderly parent. Within two weeks, a new policy was put into place to allow everyone the option of working nine or ten-hour days, four days a week, so they could take off early on Fridays. Better still, a handful were also able to shift their half days to other days of the week that were more convenient. The owner's ability to respond so quickly elevated the level of commitment and passion company-wide.

In addition, some key employees were identified for advancement, allowing the owner to take advantage of his company policy and get some of his own life back. No one had to sacrifice what was least important to what was most important in life or work, and the company's planned new division was successfully launched … in spite of everyone taking off Friday afternoons.

more than going and it isn't usually as I please!" And yet, you carry on, because even with the demands, the hassles and the pressure, you are passionate about your business.

The reality is, especially in the beginning and during any critical growth phase of a business, the entrepreneur endures unending hours, wears a hundred hats and receives poor or no pay. It becomes a balancing act — with the emphasis on "act." The only thing that keeps many business owners going is the belief that they are doing something that will make a difference and eventually produce a profit. In addition to wanting a successful business, they also desire a life outside of that business and want to enjoy the fruits of their labor. Therein lies the frustration behind the balancing act.

Too many business owners are like the vaudeville act of an entertainer feverishly spinning plates on thin lines of wire. At first he is adept at keeping the multitude of plates spinning. But he begins to find himself rushing here, there and everywhere — as one plate, and then another starts to wobble — in an effort to keep them spinning.

Does this sound like you? In the process, you start to wear out. You are doing this all on our own and you wish there were two or three others to help you keep all these plates spinning, because it's a lot of work for so little reward. Eventually a plate goes crashing to the floor — and then there is a mess to clean up.

The problem with the "balance" mindset is that it forces you to focus on what is *out* of balance. You rush to that wobbling plate to get it spinning again. When you are continuously reacting versus being proactive in your attempts to achieve this balance, you are never able to get ahead. Balance also involves adding and taking away in order to equalize, often requiring you to give something up that you may not want to. You might have fewer plates spinning, but then you feel like you are missing out on something or that you gave up too soon. When operating under this mindset, it is no wonder entrepreneurs feel pulled in a million different directions on a daily basis. But don't beat yourself up — this is how we have been conditioned for decades, if not centuries.

At one time or another, you have likely said that you have a lot of balls in the air. The problem is thinking of those "balls" as spinning plates, instead of as objects that can be caught, juggled, bounced back and tossed to someone else for a spell. Or, you may see those balls hanging in the air, like they are suspended from a mobile, and secretly hope they will stay up there until you are ready to grab them out of limbo.

Synergy feeds, nurtures and builds upon what is already in place. It is able to pull in more of what is desired with ease, at just the right moment. Synergy has each component working with the other — no more spinning out of control or being

Diagnosis for Life

The owner of a staffing firm knew all too well the sacrifices that needed to be made to build her business. Establishing her firm at the same time that she was ending a seventeen-year marriage seemed ludicrous to some. For this thirty-nine-year-old, the birthing of her business was the one thing that gave her hope and fortitude to move forward during a difficult time in her personal life. She took stock of her situation and decided she would rather triumph in building her business than "fight over dishes," so she put all of her energy into her business, stating to herself that it was a "do or die" venture.

Seven years later she had built a solid enterprise with impressive sales and profits and a staff of ten. She was dedicating about 70 to 90 hours each week to her business. She was content in doing so because her business was her life and she enjoyed the success it had realized. But her thoughts of "do or die" from all those years before came back to haunt her. One month after her business' seventh anniversary, she was diagnosed with breast cancer.

At this point it became clear that if she did not get a life in addition to her business, it was going to kill her. Fortunately, she had put some key business-saving standards into place, never fully realizing their importance — until now. She had a strong procedural system in place and had practiced what she preached to her clients by hiring good people. When she announced her diagnosis, these people stepped forward with total commitment, assuring her that the company would stay strong while she coped with her disease.

Less than a month after her diagnosis, she was in surgery, followed by fifteen months of chemotherapy. As she focused on healing, she had precious time to think about how she wanted her life to evolve. Her staff helped her realize how much she could let go of within her business. They demonstrated a level of leadership that she now recognized had been hindered by her need to be in control of every aspect of her business. She also was reminded how much she valued the wonderful friends and family members who had been there from the beginning, emotionally supporting her, and who continued to do so without pause as she battled her condition. She became grateful and aware of so many things that she had taken for granted. As she continued to heal, she also developed a deep admiration for those in the healthcare profession who had helped her battle and triumph over the cancer.

At the one year anniversary of her diagnosis of cancer, she established a second staffing company focused entirely on placing healthcare professionals. She was pleased to see that in spite of an economy in which competitors were closing offices and branches, her businesses were able to maintain their sales levels, thanks to her exceptional staff taking the reins. Slowly getting back into the business as her strength increased, she now works 45 hours, at the most, each week. She takes time for more rest and reflection, has made travel a regular escape, and enjoys friends and the outdoors.

She now cautions any business owner she comes into contact with to answer these questions: "If something were to happen to you, would your business survive, thrive or fail?" And most important of all, "Is that very same business giving you a life you love?"

Thankfully, this entrepreneur has one business that survived and is thriving, plus another business that is well on its way. She now answers the second question with total elation — "Yes!"

in limbo. Synergy doesn't force you to take away what you really want or make you feel you are ready to come crashing down. Synergy is energy. It gives you a sense of empowerment versus depleting your power.

Start thinking synergy. It will enable you to juggle your goals effortlessly by using one goal to help the other or by using resources from one goal to support the others.

EXERCISE 4:1

Do you feel as though there are some plates in your life that are ready to crash down to the floor? Answer these questions to gain perspective on your life and your business.

1. **Which activities within your life or business have your head spinning?** Why do you feel that way? Write them down. How could you leverage other resources or rally support to avoid them crashing?

2. **What would happen if these items did come crashing down?** Would it be the end of the world? Would you be able to handle and adapt? Might it be a blessing in disguise?

3. **Where are you finding the least satisfaction and greatest satisfaction in your work or life?** Why?

4. **If something were to happen to you, would your business survive, thrive or fail?** What do you need to do right now to assure it would survive or thrive, rather than fail? How can you stop spinning plates that can only be kept spinning by you?

5. **Is your business giving you a life you love, or is your entire life your business?** Look back at your personal goals. If your goals are more business-focused, go back to that Goals Mind Map and make a conscious effort to let yourself dream about a life you love. Add these new goals to the personal side.

"We don't want things spinning around us, but we have a very hard time letting go of some of the things that someone else could easily do, and perhaps even do better. It is uncomfortable to think of changing course when everything is in motion."

Chapter 5
The Juggling Entrepreneur

Watch anyone who knows how to juggle three or more balls, and they make it look easy. They have created a synergy between themselves and the balls — all working together, creating a great spectacle to watch. How great it would be to have that kind of control and ease in what we do. We are entertained by expert jugglers and enjoy the fact that they clearly consider this activity fun.

The other thing that makes jugglers so impressive is their total control of the elements being juggled. Think back to the person spinning the plates. That thin wire holding the plates has a lot of power. It puts the plates out of the person's hands for a while until he or she races back to keep another plate on top spinning. That thin wire also keeps the plates spinning in circles.

Which would you rather be, spinning in circles and feeling out of control or rising to the top? What aspects of your life or business are on a thin wire? What aspects of your life or business feel as though they are spinning out of control or just going in circles? Perhaps it is time to stop spinning and start juggling.

When juggling, the balls are always in the juggler's control. The juggler empowers the balls to be placed where he or she wants them to be placed. If one doesn't fall back into exactly the right place, it just bounces — versus crashing into a thousand pieces, like a plate — so it can be easily brought back into the flow of things without much chaos. The ball can also be tossed to someone else and then tossed back when it is ready to be returned. Some balls can be tossed away indefinitely, allowing someone else to juggle them for you. Wouldn't you rather have everyone in your company juggling balls instead of spinning plates?

As I worked on my own evolution from chaotic spinner to adept juggler, I found that I was my own worst contributor to my state of chaos. In working with clients, the same was true of them, time and time again. Chances are you know what I am talking about all too well. Are you actually getting in your own way when it comes to

LESS FOR MORE

When a nuclear plant engineer determined to go into business for himself, his desire was to work less while making more money. However, in launching his IT solutions company focused on server design, installation and support, he quickly learned that the reality was exactly opposite. He was working 50+ hours-a-week, some weeks with no salary.

Investing wisely in processes, procedures, systems and people from the very beginning, he gained some momentum in his business operations. After three years in business, he was able to take a two-week vacation with his family to Italy. When he returned he found the company had survived without him. While still working 50+ hours upon his return, he at least knew that systems were in place and he could take some time off when necessary.

Little did he know that this belief would be put to the ultimate test one year later, when his father entered the final stages of terminal cancer. The owner needed to take a projected three-to-six month leave of absence to assist his mother and family. He sat down with his operations manager to devise the best approach for this leave of absence, and the owner was prepared to offer a significant percentage of the business as incentive for the manager to take on additional responsibilities. Much to the owner's surprise, the operations manager only wanted a small percentage of the business and a final agreement was reached, allowing the owner to put his energies where needed most — with his family.

The leave of absence lasted for over five months, with the owner checking in virtually and remotely once a week, and handling paperwork or financials when needed. Much to his delight, his company grew by 20 percent over the twelve months in which he was absent for more than five of them.

The owner came to the realization that he was actually making more money by being less involved in the day-to-day operations. By default, and by trusting in those he hired to do the job, he had achieved his ultimate desire to work less and make more money. The technology, systems, procedures and processes that were put into place prior to his absence affirmed that his company could run seamlessly without him. The company had been profitable from its inception, but became even more profitable when he was less involved.

This experience allowed him to re-prioritize where he wanted to spend his time, which included more time for travel, personal and family activities. From the time he returned, he no longer put in full days and worked an average of 15 hours-a-week. He has added another manager role to complement the operations side with a strategic mindset. He continuously reassigns responsibilities among his seasoned staff so everyone can juggle effectively and keep business flowing without a hitch. His hours-per-week may increase to 20-25 hours when the company is strategically planning its next expansion, but there are no more 50+ hour weeks at no pay. There are now weeks filled with the things that make living complete and rewarding — a profitable business and a priceless ability to enjoy life to its fullest.

creating your ultimate business and life?

We don't want things spinning around us, but we have a very hard time letting go of the things that someone else could easily do, and perhaps even do better. It is uncomfortable to think of changing course when everything is in motion. We have so much riding on each of these plates that to stop them and regroup seems like time that we simply cannot afford to spend. However, as many who have successfully made the transition will attest, it is time well spent on your life and your business.

How can you start juggling and stop spinning? How can you be more in control (which we entrepreneurs rather like to be) and yet not be *out* of control in our efforts to be *in* control? How can you better define what you need to have total control of, versus what you can let go of for a while and still maintain control?

The answer to all of these questions is actually quite simple: don't feel guilty about making life easier for yourself (Promise #2); and be open to all possible support and resources (Promise #3).

EXERCISE 5:1

It's time to take a hard look at what you can delegate or eliminate. Yes, this is something you already knew needed to be done, but chances are you aren't doing it very well if you have spinning plates instead of juggling balls. Take a look at how you function as a whole. Answer these questions:

1. **Is there anything you are doing that someone else could be doing better, more efficiently or effectively?** Write these things down.

2. **Is there anything that you wish someone else were doing because you do not really like doing it?** If so, why don't you like doing it?

3. **Is there anything that you would like to be spending more time and focus on?** If so, why? What would it take to allow you to focus more on these activities?

4. **Are there aspects of your operations that can be put into a protocol, procedure, system or process so that anyone (besides you) can handle them?**

5. **Do you know the skill sets you need to hire into your business that will complement your skills so you can focus on where you can best contribute to the business?**

6. **Is there anything you or someone else is doing that could be eliminated entirely without affecting or deterring the desired end result?** Be totally open-minded about this.

7. **Are there too many steps in a particular process of doing things that could be eliminated?**

8. **Is there something you are doing in a way that is not necessarily the best or most efficient process, but you continue just because it has always been done that way?**

"From the moment we enter this world and let out our first cry, we have achieved life and are on a wonderful track of accelerated achievement for the next few short years. We are quite literally born to achieve, each and every one of us."

Chapter 6
Perception vs. Reality: Allowing Goals to Happen

Think back to the freedom we had as children to achieve without hesitation and without considering potential risks. From a very young age, we begin to achieve without knowing or understanding that we had goals. We simply decided whatever it was we were going to do and then set out to do it. As children, we achieved without understanding why or how, and everything became a learning experience. As a result, we continually progressed to a higher level.

From the time we are born, we are achieving and making phenomenal strides — almost moment by moment during those first years of life. So why should that stop as we get older? The valuable lesson that each one of us can take from our childhood, no matter what era or socioeconomic status we were born into, is that achievement is a very natural and personally gratifying experience. We are quite literally born to achieve, each and every one of us, but we are born to achieve for ourselves, not for others.

When we first are slapped into this world and let out our first cry, we have achieved life and are on a wonderful track of accelerated achievement for the next few short years: learning to grasp, walk, talk, read, write … and the list goes on. The key to our achievement at this very young and wonder filled age is in the learning. We eat, sleep and breathe the process of learning on a 24/7 basis. It comes naturally and effortlessly. We are little sponges absorbing and processing everything around us and it is completely natural, not overwhelming. We naturally live by the promises in Chapter Two. We find a way or make a way. We don't feel guilty about making life easier for ourselves. We keep our mind open to all possible resources and support.

It is when we begin to communicate with others that all sorts of limitations suddenly become part of our mindset. And where do these limitations come from?

SEEING GREEN AND LIVING IT

For years, an accomplished professional residential design specialist had been quietly incorporating sustainable living and environmentally friendly products and solutions into the million-dollar scenic homes she designed. She did this in all of her homes, even those homes in which the clients were not interested in incorporating these concepts because they considered them too costly. She knew this perception was not always correct, and she was dedicated to designing homes that exceeded clients' expectations functionally and aesthetically.

Her goal was to live in the ultimate green home, which would not only be her and her husband's dream home, but also an inspirational education center to help others discover the beauty, functional appeal and savings having a green home can bring. This had been a vision of hers for more than a decade. She saw it as a means of showcasing her design talents, while also demonstrating how to incorporate green living into any type of home. She had drafted the design and plans in hopes of seeing it come to fruition. However, there was always something that took precedence over pursuing and seeing her dream come to life.

She finally determined she was ready to pursue this dream in her nineteenth year of business. The time was right for her to finally make it happen. When she first began to share her vision, naysayers discouraged her, saying that it would be too big of a project, too consuming of her resources and too grandiose to pull off. Others were afraid to help because they had no knowledge of how to build a green home.

In spite of the daunting odds, she vowed to find a way or make a way for this house to happen. Almost immediately, the wheels started turning as she shared her vision with all those who had worked with her on countless homes before. And to her delight, they not only wanted to be a part of it, they also wanted to contribute their skills and needed materials. She was able to obtain services such as landscaping and interior design at cost. Others offered lumber, concrete, framing materials and appliances at a small percentage above cost (versus the standard cost plus 25 percent). In exchange, she offered these people exposure through promotions, articles, open home tours and broadcasts about the home while it was under construction and after its completion.

She diligently promoted her project locally, regionally and nationally. Organizations dedicated to sustainable living and green building became active in identifying all possible resources and support to help her transform a 1,200 square foot bungalow into a 4,200 square foot green home showplace. Her home has been recognized nationally as an example of how stunning and appealing living green can be, with numerous awards and exposure on national syndicated programming. The house has been used to raise money for Habitat for Humanity and is toured by hundreds of industry professionals and individuals.

In addition to creating houses for others, she has finally realized the joy of creating her own dream home — all because of a vision, a drive and a purpose that simply had to play out and come to life.

Well, not from us, but from others. As we grow older, others start to point out, from their perspective or experience, why something cannot or should not be done. Expectations by others also result in goals coming into our spheres that are not ours, but theirs.

Another aspect of our lives that begins to shape the way we approach goals is, quite frankly, when we get into a more structured learning environment. Even though we are learning, we are also being made aware of what can and cannot be done. Rules become a part of our existence, and with these rules, a mindset of limitation develops. Now this is not to say that rules are not important, because when it comes to safety and organization in group settings, they certainly have their place. The key is to take rules in the context of what they are doing as a whole versus what they are doing to you. There is something to be said for the idea that rules are meant to be broken. The key is to begin to understand your comfort level with going beyond or outside the rules and to understand when these comfort zones began to take shape.

How did you react to rules and other's perceptions as a child? Did you willingly accept them and no longer attempt something you may have otherwise tried? Did you question why? Did you rebel and do forbidden things anyway? Did you try to achieve in another way to get around the rules?

How you approach your goals today were shaped during this formative time. But it does not mean you cannot reshape them. That is the beauty of being your own person. We do have the ability to change the way we think. Your life is what your thoughts make it.

What I hope comes out of this chapter is a renewed sense of hope that you can make great strides, just like you did when you didn't know any better. The old adage, "I think I can, therefore I can" is something to embrace with all the passion you have inside. It all comes down to knowing what you truly desire and making all the pieces in your life synergize to make it happen. It also comes down to figuring out the difference between what is perceived to be an obstacle or a deterrent, and what really is one.

EXERCISE 6:1

In order to gain real perspective about your motivations and influences for achieving some goals over others, we need to explore those goals you have achieved, along with those you haven't achieved, and what each one represented to you. Answer these questions to help you better understand the dynamics of your goal achievement approach:

1. **Make a list of three things you have achieved at any time in your life personally and three things you have achieved professionally.** These should be achievements that made you feel extremely proud or personally gratified.

2. **Next to each goal, write why it was personally gratifying and how it made you feel about yourself.** What was the outcome of the achievement? What resulted in the aftermath that was also gratifying or rewarding to you personally?

3. **Now make a list of some of the goals that you wanted to achieve, but failed to achieve or ended up not pursuing.** Why? What held you back or made you decide not to pursue these things anymore? Were these reasons self-imposed or imposed upon you?

"Your greatest nemesis in achieving your goals is you. High expectations are critical in helping us succeed, but they also feed guilt, worry, pressure, impatience, dissatisfaction and other emotions that block us instead of propelling us forward to what we can ultimately realize."

Chapter 7
Self-Reflection vs. Self-Infliction: Goals in Conflict

In this chapter, we are going to do things a little differently. Take a moment to go to the end of this chapter and complete the exercise. This exercise will reveal where you are mentally before we explore Goals in Conflict. It will help you better understand your midset towards achieving both your personal and business goals.

So, where are you in the spectrum between your personal and business goals? Too personally focused? Too business focused? Downright frustrated? Accomplished, but unsatisfied? Fairly content, but wanting more? Well, clearly, you wouldn't be reading this book if everything was just peachy in your life. The real question: How do I transform my current situation from imbalance to synergy, from unsatisfied to fulfilled and from frustrated to fabulous?

First, of course, you must stop thinking of things in terms of balance. The idea of balance puts immediate pressure and guilt into your thinking, which has no place in reaching one's goals and aspirations. There is already enough pressure in just setting out to achieve a goal. Your thinking should embrace the idea of achieving synergy. And this is not pressure, but freedom. This is not guilt, but giving you permission to not feel guilty. Most importantly, it is giving you the ability to truly achieve your goals in all areas of your life.

Secondly, you must be totally honest with yourself about the goals you are working to achieve. In Chapter Three, we looked at your goals to see which ones were ones you have a passion for and which ones you were striving for out of a sense of obligation, pride or to earn someone else's approval or happiness. The goals that were not truly in your heart were more in conflict with you personally than they were in conflict with your other goals. So now is the time to officially eliminate them, if you

An Unexpected, Intentional Detour

There is nothing like a close-to-death experience to make you stop and examine your life. This was the case for an international marketing firm president who was on her way to work. On this particular day, she detoured from her regular route because of a traffic jam. Little did she know that in just minutes, she would be involved in a car accident with an eighteen wheeler. Fortunately, she was not seriously injured, but as she was helped from her car, she was profoundly grateful to be alive and immediately began pondering the meaning of why she was spared her life.

She had owned her business for eight years and was successful, and yet a small voice deep inside kept nagging at her saying, "Is this it?" She realized that out of all the work she did, what she enjoyed most was interacting with leaders and teams of people on various marketing projects. While marketing strategy, creativity and execution of a campaign was energizing, what energized her even more was getting leaders and teams fully engaged in the process. What she realized was that she no longer wanted to just work on *projects*, she wanted to be connected to life and work at a deeper, richer level by working with *people* to help them become better leaders and effective team players.

This led her to the burgeoning field of executive coaching. She enrolled in an accredited coaching program and proceeded to transition her business model. Two years later, she began offering her coaching services to her existing clients. Amazingly, eighty percent of her clients said yes. Today she uses the knowledge of her global marketing and advertising experience with executives from around the world, thus bringing the best of her past into her present entrepreneurial endeavor of leadership consulting and coaching.

Who would have guessed that a detour from the regular path would have led her to work that makes her feel alive, joyful and grateful. Her business is profitable in not only the monetary sense, but in making a true and lasting difference as well.

haven't already. From here forward, they are no longer to be considered. Remember our second promise from Chapter Two? "I will not feel guilty about making life easier on myself."

By releasing these goals, you are freeing your mind of the balance-ridden guilt that comes with obligation, pride or being responsible for someone else's happiness. One of the biggest strides I made in my journey towards synergy was realizing that I couldn't be the vessel for other people's happiness. If someone else's happiness is totally dependent on you, then this person needs to read this book! Happiness is generated from within and flows outward. You don't attract happiness; you radiate happiness.

Let's take a look at those of you who are too business focused, as this is most likely the majority of you. I certainly have been a victim of this, so understanding the whys of this particular dilemma is near and dear to my heart. The reality is that when you first start a business, you will be more business focused out of the sheer necessity to get it off the ground. So if you are in a start-up mode with your business, you can stop beating yourself over the head about being so focused on your business, because it is necessary.

Having been in business for twenty five years, my business is older than any of my children. This brings to point a wonderful analogy. I was raising a business and children at the same time, both of which I consider my offspring. Your business, whether you have children or not, is your offspring of your creation. So let's consider this for a moment.

During the first few years of raising children, they are totally dependent on you for everything. You must cater to their every need — from nourishment to nurturing. Your business is no different. It is totally dependent on you to take its first steps. As a child grows, he or she gains more self-assurance and some independence. Your child still needs you, but in small incremental ways. This is the same for your business.

As your business begins to take shape and move beyond its first stage of infancy, you begin to see it is a viable business and some aspects of it continue to flow along *with* you, versus *because* of you. More people begin to interact with your children as they grow and hopefully, they are positive influences. The same is true for your business as it grows. More people are interacting with it, including employees, suppliers, vendors, clients and advisors. They are ideally going to have a positive influence on its growth, taking some of the stress off of your shoulders.

The critical juncture is if you are still too heavily business focused even when you are not the only one involved in your business. Why is this happening? For me, it was because my business was where I received satisfaction, so it served as my wonderful escape from what was not satisfying in my personal life. The funny thing is that while my business was my refuge, I was also holding myself back from what my business could be. My life was in conflict instead of synergy.

Is this the case with you? Are you using your business as an escape versus another part of what makes your life complete? If so, it is time to take a look at your personal life and see what is not working and why, and then move forward to synergize. We will begin this process in later chapters. Just realizing this right now is what truly matters.

Now let's look at those of you who are too personally focused. Unless you are in a lifestyle business, the likelihood of you as an entrepreneur being too personally focused is small. The majority of entrepreneurs are too business focused. This is something that doesn't take a lot of analysis to see. However, there is the case where entrepreneurs can find themselves being too personally focused and justify this by calling their business a lifestyle business.

The whole concept of having a lifestyle business has come into vogue over the last decade as a result of, once again, a desire to create balance in one's life. People who own a lifestyle business claim it is not driven by profit or growth, but by a personal choice to get off the fast track in order to have a more balanced life. My premise is that this is hurting people because deep inside they really want to do more. While they profess to be in a lifestyle business in order to spend more time with family, friends, hobbies and so on, they have underlying unfulfilled areas of their life, either personally or professionally, that just can never seem to get off the ground.

Now before I explore this further, I want to say that there is a case for having a lifestyle business, without any huge aspirations of grandeur. Some people are perfectly satisfied and fulfilled in working for themselves and making enough to live on. These people are not being any less than they can be. They are perfectly content and are likely not as goals-driven as those of you reading this book. They also may have already achieved a great deal and are now ready to slow the pace down a bit. They no longer have anything to prove to themselves. They can now enjoy the fruits of their labor and still enjoy some stimulation and challenge, but in a different realm. No one says you have to be goals-driven or achievement-driven. There is nothing wrong with you if you are not, as long as you are happy. So let's not get into some imposing mindset that those without a continuous stream of goals are somehow missing out. It is all about choice and once again, whatever makes a person feel happy and fulfilled.

But more likely, you are reading this book because your desire to achieve is in conflict with the idea of a lifestyle business and you are still struggling with balance in your life. If you are being totally honest with yourself right now, you still feel out of balance, don't you? Even though the outside world perceives and perhaps envies your lifestyle, you know there is something still missing. This creates immense pressure to continue to live up to this professed state of being, doesn't it? You may even worry about what it will look like if you falter.

So what do you do when you are able to achieve *your* idea of balance but still feel unfulfilled? Then you need to stop thinking balance and start thinking synergy!

EXERCISE 7:1

Before you can begin to bring synergy into your life and work, you need to know where you are right now in your attempts to balance so you can shift your mindset and take true action. Check the statements below, which apply to you, then reference the key on the next page:

❑   1.   **I have specific personal goals unrelated to business.**

❑   2.   **I have determined action steps to achieve my personal goals.**

❑   3.   **I have specific business/career goals, both long term and short term.**

❑   4.   **I have a strategy for helping me achieve these business/career goals.**

❑   5.   **I am more successful at reaching my business/career goals.**

❑   6.   **I am more successful at reaching my personal goals.**

❑   7.   **I am not achieving either my business/career or personal goals to my satisfaction.**

❑   8.   **Because of my personal goals, I accept that I cannot fully realize my business/career goals at this time.**

❑   9.   **Because of my business/career goals, I accept that I cannot fully realize my personal goals at this time.**

❑   10.   **I am content, but there are still aspects of my life and work that I know could be even better.**

❑   11.   **I don't have any specific personal goals. I'm totally focused on my business/career at this time.**

❑   12.   **I reach my personal and business/career goals, but it still isn't enough.**

Is this an accurate description of how you feel?

If you checked 3,4,5,9,11 . . . . too business focused, affecting personal life
You need to stop thinking you must sacrifice your life for work. And chances are your family and friends have already been telling you this. Sacrifice is a balancing mindset.

If you checked 1,2,6,8 . . . . . . too personally focused, affecting business/career success
Even if your personal life has posed many demands upon you, it doesn't mean you cannot have business/career success too. If you think you have no choice but to choose one over the other right now, then you are in a balancing mindset versus a synergy mindset. You are pitting one against the other.

If you checked 1,3,7 and 2 or 4, 8 or 9 . . . . frustrated and getting nowhere
To you, these goals are still just dreams. While you have goals, that is as far as you have taken it. You are likely feeling overwhelmed, which is a balancing mindset. If you don't know where to begin, consider your reasons for your goals and start putting some action steps and strategies into place based on these reasons.

If you checked 1,2,3,4,7 . . . . . . achievement focused, but not achieving what's desired
You are likely in a constant tug of war between both personal and business/career, and so nothing is getting accomplished in your eyes. You do a little here and a little there, but are not seeing any real progress. You thought you were doing it right, but it feels like you are shifting gears between life and work whenever you take action in one area or another. They still are separate in your mind. Feeling this way is a balancing mindset.

If you checked 1,2,3,4,10 . . . . content, but want more
You can't complain. You feel fortunate in many ways, but there are things you still want to accomplish and still want to do. Who you are or the things that you are most passionate about have not been fully realized and explored. It is likely you have a fear that you will lose balance in your life.

If you checked 1,2,3,4,12 . . . . accomplished, yet unsatisfied
It may be that you have played it a little too safe because of a balancing mindset. There are goals that just seem so "out there" and so "bodacious" that you have convinced yourself they are beyond reach. It is also possible you may be ready for something totally different to challenge you.

"Why does conflict exist in our lives or business to begin with? Because whatever the conflicts may be, they are typically going against what we believe, value or stand for. Sometimes we don't exactly even know what it is, but we know it does not feel right."

Chapter 8
From Conflict to Purpose

Now that you have validated that you are either too business focused, too personally focused, frustrated, discouraged or unsatisfied with what you have achieved, let's do something about your current state. It is time to leave the whole idea of balance behind and get you on your journey towards synergy.

Part of the problem is in how we have approached goals, beyond just compartmentalizing them as either business or personal. Another challenge is having numerous goals that have nothing that ties them together, either in our minds or our lives. They are random desires with no connections that would strengthen them and enable you to build one upon the other. Remember the definition of synergy: the interaction or cooperation of two or more forces so that their combined effect is greater than the sum of their individual effects. Beginning to see and act upon how your goals can work together instead of against one another will put you on the threshold of a whole new way of approaching your life and work ... through synergy.

To begin this process, two distinctive aspects of how you think, live and work must be considered in more depth to help you achieve like you have never achieved before. The first is to take a look at the personal values that dictate how you operate in life and in business. The second is to take a look at what you believe your ultimate purpose is — as a person and within your business.

In an entrepreneurial company, the company's culture and values are driven by the owner. Your personal values naturally become your business values. The entrepreneur is the inspiration behind the company and all it represents. Anyone who works there needs to share these same values, or it doesn't work. Even if the values have not been blazoned into the business plan or on the company website, they exist in action everyday — by what you as the owner expect, direct, declare and profess in everything you do.

BEYOND MISSION

One month after September 11, 2001, the CEO of a successful accounting practice serving public and private sector companies was hit with another tragedy — a father who was diagnosed with cancer. As the oldest daughter, the owner needed to take some time off as her father's cancer progressed to help tend to family needs with her sisters and mother. This resulted in her spending considerable time away from the business in order to be there for her family.

At the end of 2002, she received a wake-up call when revenues for her business were down 42 percent. The fallout from 9-11, along with her reduced focus on her business due to the family crisis, had negatively impacted the business more significantly than she had anticipated. The reality was that her company was too reliant on her involvement in operations and bringing in new business. Her team was not embracing what she was trying to do in the business. They could not take her ideas and run with them unless she was there. At this time, she began questioning the real purpose of her business and why her team was not acting on the mission she thought she had conveyed.

Through the help of an executive coach, she began the process of revisiting her mission and vision for the company. But she kept getting stuck. Nothing was feeling right because it seemed like something everyone else had done before. She went home and began to think of what she really wanted her company to represent, and then the true purpose and difference her business could make became clear.

It was more than a mission and a vision. Her purpose was to leave a legacy and operate with genuine intentions in everything that her company and its people did to serve clients, the community and themselves. She determined that the legacy her company would leave is one in which Corporate America is better served when professionals honor their lives. From there, she defined intentions for the working environment and the firm's relationship with its clients and people.

Where other accounting firms expected staff to work unending hours at pivotal times of the year, her firm would delight its people by maintaining normal working hours so their personal lives could be enjoyed. Her firm would build genuine relationships with clients that make a positive, long-lasting and measurable difference in their businesses. She also would honor her own life by delegating and releasing areas that others were willing and capable of handling on her behalf.

When she introduced her new Legacy and Intentions to her team, they embraced it and continued to build upon what it meant to them, the company and its clients. This energized the owner and the firm as a whole. It also set standards for attracting clients and team members who embraced this same philosophy toward business and life.

The owner keeps the Legacy and Intentions alive, thriving and evolving. At quarterly meetings, she continuously reinforces them and her teams explore how they can best serve clients, each other and their communities. The firm has grown to three offices and more than 55 people serving clients across the Southeast. It has been recognized as a statewide Top-100 Small Business, an Inc. Magazine Fast Growth Company, a Top-40 Family-Friendly Company and a Financial Impact Leader — proving that honoring lives reaps rewards and awards for business well done.

Understanding your values and what is at the core of who you are, and therefore, how the company does business, is critical to achieving more and distinguishing your business within your marketplace. Oftentimes conflicts arise due to core values being challenged or ignored. Could it be that the reason that you are either too personally focused or too business focused is because there are some values being challenged? If you do not feel honored in either your personal or business life, you will not enjoy being involved in that aspect of your life.

Upon understanding your values more clearly, you may also see where a goal is not in alignment with one of your values, and therefore, should be eliminated or reassessed. A personal example is that years ago I had a goal to be a certain weight. This became a continuous plague to me. My reason for setting this goal, was that someone else in my life thought I should be at this particular weight and I wanted to make that person happy. My values of unconditional love and acceptance were being challenged. Upon re-evaluating my goals, I chose not to eliminate this particular one, because I did want to be in better shape, but instead I modified it to what would make *me* happy.

My new goal became to create a leaner, healthier body for greater energy and endurance. It was no longer about weight or how I looked for others, but how it would make me feel and what it would enable me to do. Much more in line with my values, I embraced this goal as my own and I continue to realize its benefits on a daily basis as my body gets stronger and my energy continues to soar higher. And guess what? It has had a profound effect on my ability to focus and impact my business goals as well.

Along with your values, you should also consider your personal purpose and the ultimate purpose of your business. It might be easiest to start with your business, as typically a business will have a mission statement. What does your mission statement say about your business and its purpose? Does it go to a higher level of being or is it simply professing what you do, reading more like a glorified capabilities statement? If it just says what you do, then you are not really sharing a purpose or mission.

I determined that my company's mission is to create more savvy marketers out of small business owners and their employees. This mission was determined years ago, and has resulted in such innovation compared to others in my industry that we have been honored for our unique approach multiple times on a local, national and international level. My personal mission is to inspire and motivate change and new ways of thinking and perceiving. I truly believe I was put on earth to do this, and therefore, every choice that I make is based on how I can accomplish this on a variety of fronts, both personally and professionally.

A mission is about what you are continually striving to do, not just what you are doing. Your ultimate purpose helps you get at the mission in business and in life, and then becomes intertwined in your mind, your heart, your actions and your words. If you have a purpose and are on a true mission to fulfill this purpose, then what results is an explosion of opportunity. That's because you are no longer limiting yourself within the confines of how you are doing business now, but how you could be doing business to continually enhance your ability to fulfill your mission.

On the personal side, if you can pinpoint where you can make the biggest difference with your natural talents or skills or what you are most passionate about, all of a sudden you see relationships you never noticed before. These can facilitate you making that difference. Best of all, by knowing what both your personal and business missions are, you are synergizing your way to a whole new level of happiness and achievement.

EXERCISE 8:1

It's time to look both inside yourself and inside your business to see what makes them thrive from a values and purpose standpoint. Answer these questions:

1. **What is your personal philosophy on how life should be lived?**

2. **What values do you hold dear and believe should never be compromised for any reason?**

3. **What are some characteristics or practices of others that you consider undesirable or unacceptable and why?**

4. **What do you hope you give to or inspire in others by what you do and say?**

5. **What do you need and desire in your life and work to feel fulfilled and happy?**

6. **How have you incorporated your values into how you do business and how you do business differently from others?**

7. **What are your beliefs about how a business should operate and how does this relate to how you think your personal life should also operate?**

EXERCISE 8:2

Now that you have taken time to identify your values, it is time to transfer them to a Values Mind Map so that you can view them as a big picture in a more organized way. Just as you created a Goals Mind Map, you are now going to create a Values Mind Map that depicts your values in both life and business, all together for you to see.

Take another 11" x 17" ledger size sheet or paper from a flip chart pad to begin capturing your values based on the diagram below. Use the Values Guide and Examples on the next page as reference to place items in the right place on your Values Mind Map. You will define the following:

- Value
- Who shares this value
- Reasons for your value
- Ultimate benefit of the value
- How your value may be in conflict or be challenged

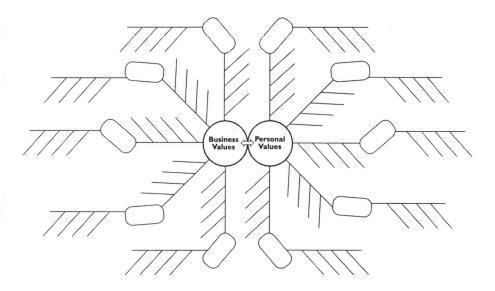

Values Guide and Examples

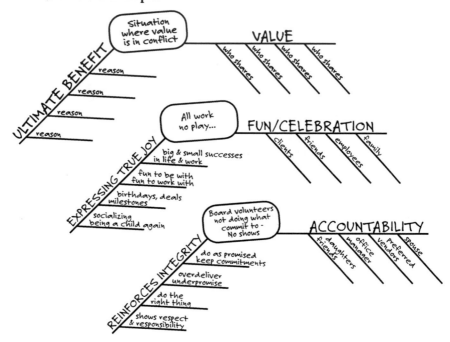

Now that your values are captured on your Mind Map, look at your values beyond what they are — to what they mean to you. Take a look at why they are important to you and the ultimate benefit you realize from having these values. Identify those values which may be in conflict, how they are currently in conflict or are being challenged in some way. Then consider how the ones currently in conflict may be affecting your ability to reach certain goals.

NOTE: You can also go to **www.MeMyselfandInc.com** and order downloadable templates to be printed on 11 x 17 paper, or hard copies to be mailed to you.

EXERCISE 8:3

Answer these questions to help you define your personal and business purpose:

1. For you personally, what do you enjoy doing or how do you enjoy being more than anything else in the world?

2. When do you feel you are making a real difference? How does this impact others and make you feel as a result?

3. What is the one thing that makes you passionate and excited? How can you use this in creating your ultimate purpose?

4. For your business, what is your company ultimately trying to do for the markets it serves?

5. What is the difference your business is trying to make for your customer or consumer that no other company is currently doing as well or at all?

6. What are you trying to prove can be done that has not been done in quite the same way before in your industry?

7. What legacy would you like your business to leave behind as a result of its existence?

"Finally accepting the fact that your business and personal lives must co-exist is the first critical step toward truly synergizing your world into your ultimate reality."

Chapter 9
Business and Personal: Putting It All Together

In Chapter One, you composed both your personal and business goals for the first time within one large Goals Mind Map. This may have been an uncomfortable exercise for you. This exercise was intentionally created to force you to stop separating and compartmentalizing your personal and business goals as separate parts of your life, and help you begin to see them as being related within your life.

In Chapter Three, you determined which goals represented your passions and which ones were perhaps based on the expectations of someone else. This may very well have caused you to create a new Mind Map, eliminating some goals that your heart never embraced in the first place, and keeping or adding goals that reflect where you truly desire to be headed.

In Chapters Six, Seven and Eight, you explored goals that appear to be in conflict and learned how your attitude, mindset and focus needs to shift to allow these goals to exist and thrive together, as a result of synergizing them through a clear understanding of your values and purpose.

Take a look at your Mind Map. Notice how it resembles an intricate spider's web. Everything in your life is and should be connected, just like the strands of a spider's web. Your personal and business goals should be connected because it is likely that some of the actions you need to take will interweave to help you achieve all your goals more easily and efficiently. Viewed together, they become a stronger possibility. Planned together, they become a distinct probability.

How does this work? Gaining a holistic view of your personal and business goals powerfully connects them within your mind to help you make new connections you would have otherwise never made. You will also have finally crossed over the threshold of accepting the fact that your business and personal life must co-exist. And

Frequent Flyer Smiles

The owner of a high-end, by appointment only retail fashion business had the personal long-term goal of gaining more time and money to travel for pleasure, and a short-term goal to increase profits in the business. Her business goals also included expanding the designer lines she was featuring in her boutique. This would mean more frequent trips to New York, adding expense that would eat into her profits initially.

By keeping an open mind, she was able to devise a solution that helped her achieve even more than she could have imagined. She discovered that many of the designer houses that supplied her inventory and special order clothing offered the option of payment by credit card. Once she realized the advantages of this, she secured credit cards with frequent flier miles. With tens of thousands of dollars worth of clothing inventory and orders being charged to these cards on a seasonal basis, the owner quickly accumulated more than enough miles to not only cover frequent trips to New York, but to cover travel for personal pleasure. In addition, as a result of the savings realized from no longer having to pay business travel expenses, the owner was able to afford to bring on a part-time assistant. This enabled her to take some personal time off and helped keep her business running while she was on buying trips or away from the boutique.

The owner, who now frequently enjoys travel for pleasure, was able to realize her long-term personal goal in the short-term. Not only did she realize more profits for her business, but she was able to hire some much needed help sooner than originally planned.

with this realization, you have made the first critical step toward truly synergizing your world into *your* ultimate reality. Then you can start to better assess what you need, what your options are and what your next steps can be. This is also a good time to remind you of the three promises in Chapter Two you made to yourself: finding a way or making a way; not feeling guilty about making life easier for yourself; and being open to all possible resources and support.

To illustrate this, let me share a personal experience. When I was pregnant with my third daughter, I desired to continue to grow my business, while also spending more time with my three daughters. These goals were clearly in conflict for me. I desired more time with my daughters because the business seemed to be consuming me more than I wanted it to, and now another child was entering my life. With a third child on the way, it was even more important that somehow I achieve more time for all of my daughters, and yet I still wanted to grow my business. By looking at these goals together and assessing the overall situation, I determined that I needed an office manager for my business. This allowed me to delegate aspects of my business that were consuming my time and that I did not enjoy anyway, allowing me to recapture time to achieve my personal goals. It required me to be willing to give up a measure of control by allowing someone else to handle aspects of my business. But the end result was well worth it.

Now it's time for you to re examine your goals using this new mindset. Take a look at your reasons for your goals, your expected outcomes, who is impacted and what people or resources are needed. You will find yourself more readily making associations between one goal and another. You will start to see goals that impact the same people or goals that may require the support of the same type of people. You will look at those goals that appear to be in conflict in a new way. Before you know it, they are no longer in conflict as you find solutions and options you never considered before. You will start to look at your long-term and short-term goals on both sides and begin to consider how they can work together to achieve the long-term faster and the short-term easier. You will no longer have a business plan separate from your personal life, but a *life plan* that gets down to the business of helping you realize what you ultimately want to realize in your lifetime.

Smooth Sailing

A couple who owned a variety of real estate investments in a business had a short-term business goal of using their profits to diversify their investment opportunities. Their long-term personal dream was to eventually own a yacht and sail around the world when they retired.

Their creative financial planner helped them realize the dream of owning their yacht in the present — through the same concept that had built their property investment business. They used their profits as a down payment on a yacht, which could be rented for weeks at a time, just as one would rent a beach house or mountain home. They were able to enjoy the yacht on weeks it was not rented. It paid for itself and made further profits through the rental program. By the time the couple retires, they will be able to afford an even larger yacht than the one they had envisioned. The couple's life plan allowed them to begin living the dream of owning a yacht right now.

EXERCISE 9:1

As you glance over your Goals Mind Map, you may have already begun to associate how your goals could potentially work together in a holistic way. You may have also been inspired by the examples to open up your thinking to more creative solutions. To help see the possibilities, assess your goals as follows:

1. **Get out some highlighters.** Highlight similar reasons for your goals in one color, and highlight similar resources or people needed in another color. Study the similarities to see how they could possibly work together. How can you leverage the same resources to achieve all that you are setting out to do? What expert or adviser might you need to bring in who could help you look at these goals in unison and offer some creative solutions based on the resources needed?

2. **Reference the matrix below.** Place your short-term personal goals alongside your long-term business goals and your long-term personal goals alongside your short-term business goals. See if you can make any connections.

Personal-ST	Business / Career-LT
1. _____	_____
2. _____	_____
3. _____	_____

Personal-LT	Business / Career-ST
1. _____	_____
2. _____	_____
3. _____	_____

" Real or imagined, an excuse or a reality, imposed or predisposed — whatever is occurring that seems to be keeping you from where you want to be personally or professionally is all a matter of what you believe and accept. "

SECTION 2

Overcoming What Holds You Back

Over many years of observing and working with entrepreneurs, I've heard it all. So many people are on the cusp of their greatness or happiness, but are not able to get there because they believe a situation to be out of their control or simply the way that it is. This line of thinking falls into two distinct categories — wishful thinking and fearful thinking.

Wishful thinking sounds like this: "If only I had more…" Have you caught yourself wishing for more options, confidence, time, money, support or resources?

Then, of course, there is that uncomfortable mindset that exists when we venture into anything new or foreign. That's fearful thinking. So what are you afraid of? Could you be afraid of letting someone down, failure, success, losing control, taking risks, boredom or being ordinary?

Real or imagined, an excuse or a reality, imposed or predisposed — whatever is occurring that seems to be keeping you from where you want to be personally or professionally is all a matter of what you believe and accept. The ability to look inside yourself and acknowledge those aspects that keep you from making progress toward your goals is the first step toward finally realizing your ultimate life.

These next chapters are dedicated to helping you uncover, discover and recover from your mental demons and exorcise them once and for all. Problems will no longer be viewed as obstacles, but opportunities. Your current mindset, including those things that were not clear to you until now, will crystallize.

You will read about others who have succeeded, simply by putting their wishful and fearful thinking aside. They put the three promises to powerful use by tackling each mental perception once and for all. You will come out of this section full of possibilities. You will see yourself and how you think in a new light. You will better understand what motivates you and what holds you back. This kind of wisdom can only mean one thing — utter and total success. Now that is exciting, isn't it?

"You set high expectations for yourself and hold yourself to a higher standard than most. High expectations are what can also hold you back from truly taking your enterprise to its next level."

Chapter 10
Letting Go What Enslaves You

The moment you start your business, you set upon a course of self-enslavement. Somehow it isn't so bad in the beginning, even with the long hours and the amazing number of hats that you wear. There is a level of intention surrounding your venture that keeps you going strong for quite some time. You went into business knowing there would be a certain amount of sacrifice, but you didn't mind, as the end result would be worth it. You set high expectations for yourself and hold yourself to a higher standard than most. This is part of what makes you so driven to succeed in owning and building your own business. High expectations are what can also hold you back from truly taking your enterprise to its next level.

The idea of perfection in anything is deceptive, because reaching perfection is a never-ending pursuit. Striving for it, however, has merit as long as you don't put your life or business on hold in the process. Your determination to "get it just right" before the next phase can be unleashed is admirable, as long as it is justified. How many of you are on the cusp of launching something new, but still haven't gotten it exactly the way you want it before putting it out there for the world to see? As you continue to focus on getting it to the point where you *think* it needs to be, is your conviction actually enslaving you to the point of inactivity? The key is accepting that you are on a course of continuous improvement. Once you see this and start thinking in this vein, you will begin to see progress again and the rewards that come with it.

As time goes on and the business actually does begin to grow and others get involved in helping make the products or services happen, the entrepreneur often continues to feel enslaved to the business and the obligations that come with it. In spite of having a team or resources to rely upon, the entrepreneur is still the one that must keep every aspect of the business flowing because he or she knows specific things that no-one else seems to know. You are so busy in the day-to-day of your business, you don't have time to think about its future. If every aspect of your business

From Logistical Slave to Free Visionary

A sporting events and entertainment company president and CEO was a slave to his own business, even though there were eight dedicated and passionate staff members ready and willing to do whatever it took to put on award-winning events that wowed clients. Why? Because he was still the only one anyone could go to whenever an event was in its planning and execution stages. All of the resources and logistics associated with putting on the event effortlessly were in his head. Whenever decisions needed to be made, he had to be involved.

Not only was this causing frustration on the part of those trying to get the work done, but it was resulting in the entrepreneur literally working night and day to be available to his employees to answer any and all questions related to any given event. He was consumed by his business in the day-to-day. He had no time to think about a long-term business strategy that would assure his business continued on its course as a leader in the professional sports entertainment arena. The entrepreneur was working himself to exhaustion and his family shared his frustration.

Through the assistance of an entrepreneurial coach, the owner began to let go by taking the knowledge base that was in his head and downloading it into systems, procedures and reference materials. This meant that others could handle events without the need for his continuous involvement. Over a six-month period, he made a concentrated effort to analyze and document exactly how he made his events company so effective in order to systematize various operations for others to manage.

The end result was that his business evolved from being a company that was owner-directed to a company with a visionary owner and a management team that efficiently directed and managed day-to-day operations. In addition, a logistics manager was brought on board to oversee all aspects and serve as the point person for events. The company has many more awards under its belt and has grown to an impassioned staff of more than seventy-eight team members. Most important of all, the owner has his life back. He can now stay one step ahead strategically because others are handling the day-to-day business.

still relies on you to keep it going, then it is time to start letting go. By letting go of the need to be involved in every aspect of your company's operations, you can focus on where your business is headed, versus how it is functioning each and every minute.

A situation that can also take its toll and be a detriment to a business owner is over-committing to a myriad of obligations inside and outside of the business. This is probably the occurrence I see the most. My firm conducted research comparing high-growth companies to companies with stagnant or negative growth. We found that owners of companies with high growth limited their involvement in organizations, while no-growth companies had business owners over-involved, taking their focus away from their business and making them less productive. The reality for the no-growth owners is they couldn't say no. They were under the guise that their involvement in these organizations was good for business, when it may well not have been.

Your personal life is no different. If you have convictions on the business side, you also have similar and strong convictions on the personal side. This places you in the predicament of enslavement as you try to live up to your own expectations and ideals. This in turn can create an internal conflict in how you approach both your business and your personal life as you try to keep all of your ideals, beliefs and personal expectations in check.

I found that my strong belief in keeping my commitments, specifically personal commitments, was actually becoming the very thing that was holding me back on a variety of levels. I was unhappy in my personal life and how it was continuing to evolve. I was guilt-ridden at some of the obligations I no longer wanted to keep, and was finding myself longing for what was missing.

One New Year's Day, I read a book in which a particular statement jumped out at me and awoke me to what I was doing to myself. It helped me to see that living up to my word and my expectations of myself were enslaving me more than I realized. In looking at my values as a whole, I began to see that my value of commitment was affecting and superseding other values. In trying to live up to my expectation and these obligations, I was actually sacrificing or putting aside other values in the process — hence my unhappiness. In that moment, I knew exactly what I needed to do. I needed to keep the promise to myself about not feeling guilty about making life easier for myself. Why? Because my unhappiness in my personal life also had a direct effect on how I was approaching my business.

Due to my unhappiness on the personal front, I became a perpetual workaholic. My business was where I was finding satisfaction, gratification and camaraderie in my

THE GRACIOUS GOURMET

The owner of a specialty catering and meals preparation company was doing all the things a start-up does to get noticed and get her company's name known. Among her strategies was getting involved on the boards and committees of civic and business organizations, as well as offering free samples to give people a taste of her products. While the initial thrust of these strategies seemed effective, it began to consume both her time and her business profits. The end result was that she became a slave to her volunteer obligations and promotional efforts, to the detriment of her paying clients and the launch of the meal preparation portion of her business.

When she took a step back to analyze her many involvements, she realized that some were not a good match with those clients her business best served. However, she did not want to jeopardize her reputation as someone who honored her commitments. She identified some indirect competitors in a start-up phase that would be willing to take the same approach and were a better fit for these organizations. This worked like a charm. The organizations were impressed that instead of simply resigning, she took it upon herself to find replacements, and her competitors thought her gracious for sharing these opportunities.

She kept a couple of her community involvements that made sense because they were a good match for her catering business. She then identified a group that could foster awareness and opportunity for her meal preparation business. As a result, she also gained a valuable future partner to assist with this new aspect of her business.

Finally, she determined that her free samples needed to be budgeted and tracked just like any other expense or investment in a business. From that point forward, instead of offering samples carte blanche to a group, she offered them for a pre-selected event or function and then presented special offers, good only to those in attendance.

Not long after this shift, and as her business continued to grow, she no longer needed to offer freebies. She now enjoys mentoring others starting in the business on how to effectively use her promotional tactic. Fortunately for them, they won't have to learn the hard way like she did.

efforts, so I put all my focus and attention into it. But this, in turn, had an impact on another value of mine, which was spending more time with my family. Looking back, I realize that because of my unhappiness on one side, I created busy work rather than efforts that produced significant strides within my company, just to have something to do to distract me from my other unhappy situation. I was confusing activity with achievement and so was not achieving what I could have with a more focused and less stressed mindset.

Do you find yourself either avoiding your life or avoiding your business because it is not exactly the way you want it to be, or because of outside commitments and obligations? Remember Promise #2: Don't feel guilty about making life easier for yourself. This promise is one that you need to keep reminding yourself of as you take a look at all of the things that are enslaving you. It will allow you to let them go or redirect them to be on purpose, rather than having them weigh heavily on your psyche.

EXERCISE 10:1

Are there any projects or initiatives you are currently working on in your business that have not been launched for the rest of the world to see? If yes, then list them and then answer these questions:

1. **When do you expect to officially introduce the initiative?** Have you set an introduction or launch date? If not, why not?

2. **Are you finding that you are holding it up because of a desire to make it better, higher quality, or something else?** What are these reasons and are they really going to make or break its success for a launch? Could it be launched and continually improved?

3. **If you moved forward with introducing this as it currently is, what would be the worst that could happen?** Is this scenario a true possibility or simply an excuse to keep holding it back?

4. **What made you start the initiative in the first place?** Is this still valid and appropriate for where your business is currently?

5. **Are there other initiatives or projects you have on the back burner that could be more important, but you believe this one must be launched first?** If it is no longer as important, could it be that it is in this quagmire because your passion is no longer in it?

6. **What would happen if you abandoned this project or initiative?** Could abandoning it altogether actually free you to focus on more relevant work?

7. **If it is still deemed of value and merit, could other resources be pulled in to help bring it to completion?**

EXERCISE 10:2

Are there any commitments that you have made either personally or professionally that you find are no longer enjoyable, satisfying or that you simply dread, yet believe that you must fulfill because of your strong sense of obligation and doing as promised? If yes, list them and then answer these questions:

1. **Why did you make the commitment in the first place?** Was it truly centered from *your* desire or someone else's?

2. **Is this a commitment that holds great significance in your life but has changed unexpectedly?** How has it changed, and what has come to be as a result?

3. **Are any of your other values being sacrificed as a result of this obligation being fulfilled?** What are they?

4. **Are any of your other values being sacrificed as a means of avoiding or distracting yourself from the reality of this unsatisfying or unfulfilling commitment?**

5. **Is there a way to refocus this commitment to better align it with what you can be passionate about or motivated to fulfill?** Restate it now and see if this makes a difference. If you cannot restate it, then it may be time to let it go.

6. **Is there someone else who could take over this commitment and therefore fulfill the promise without you having to be ultimately responsible?**

"The most effective entrepreneurs are also great managers of their destiny. They know how to get things done beyond the confines of their minds and their capabilities, and as a result, they make more effective decisions when choices need to be made."

Chapter 11
Choices, Choices Everywhere

An entrepreneur's passion for ideas, invention and innovation can be a challenge. We are always thinking, and as a result, we are always coming up with new things to add to our already busy lives. Herein lies one of the key problems with many entrepreneurs and their ability to reach their goals effectively. Not only are we bombarded with choices to be made in the day-to-day existence of our businesses and lives, but we ourselves add to the bombardment with a continuous stream of ideas, options, insights and the next great thing.

For some, this is information overload of our own making, which leaves us not knowing which option to focus on in order to move forward. Does this sound like you? You may feel like the little ball in the pinball machine, bouncing back and forth to each option to touch it for a little while but not really ever landing on it to see it through to completion. Or perhaps you are the type that simply puts ideas in the "get to it later" realm because you must finish this one thing first. The problem is that these notions nag at you in the depths of your subconscious and continue to rise back up and remind you they are there and ask you why you aren't doing something with them. As a result, the one thing you are trying to get done is not receiving your full attention and is dragging on until it becomes not as much fun. So then you pull one of the other things out of your realm of options and focus on it for a while. Still nothing is seeing itself to completion.

Now there is nothing wrong with having a plethora of options and ideas, as this is what makes being an entrepreneur exciting. But if we allow our thinking to paralyze our ability to take action, then it is a problem that needs to be addressed. It can lead to frustration and a feeling that nothing is getting done. And we entrepreneurs do not like that feeling. We like to have a clear direction and know the road we need to take to get us there. As Will Rogers said, "The road to success is dotted with many tempting parking places."

Profit Sizing

An international warranty company was going through major growing pains as a result of a recent acquisition to expand its footprint throughout North America. Its workforce spanned many years with the company, and everyone from the CEO to the front line was being spread thin, putting in major hours to satisfy the many markets they served. The company was also undergoing major infrastructural changes to accommodate expansion and more sophisticated communication requirements.

As management (including two company founders) started to see frustrations increase company-wide, their focus shifted to taking a hard look at the decisions necessary to bring everything into equilibrium for the company and its dedicated employees.

First, with the help of a strategic marketing consultant, the management team realized that part of the reason everyone was spread so thin was because they were serving too many markets. Some were no longer as profitable and were taking energy away from those that were. Some of these less profitable markets had helped build the company during its earlier years, so there was an emotional attachment, especially by the founders. Going through an exercise that weighed each market based on profitability, needed resources and long-term opportunities quickly showed the founders that these markets were draining the company and its employees.

Second, management took a look at what was draining the team in-house and identified better qualified outside resources to help alleviate the load. As a result of these two critical initiatives, everyone profited. Employees got portions of their lives back. At work, they were able to focus their energies where they felt the most competent and able to contribute. The company profited by no longer trying to serve markets that were no longer serving them, enabling them to more effectively build an infrastructure dedicated to future growth, and based on sound strategy and focus.

The reason why you feel like you're stuck in a parking place is because you are trying to do, oversee, facilitate and control everything. This can stop you dead in your tracks. That parking place is more like a traffic bottleneck. Sometimes you need to have the faith to let go of some critical things to allow other individuals to keep them going. As an effective entrepreneurial juggler, you have now handed off one of your balls. When it comes back to you, it can take on a whole new realm of energy as it moves back into play within your big picture. This is synergy, and it is invigorating.

The most effective entrepreneurs are also great managers of their destiny. They know how to get things done beyond the confines of their minds and their capabilities, and as a result, they make more effective decisions when choices need to be made. Part of the problem with having many options, choices and ideas is that they are all still only a part of you and only you.

Several years ago, I was listening to the author Mary Cantando, who spoke at a meeting I was attending. I was feeling like there were so many things I had going or that could be going, but nothing was moving forward. As we often do at this stage of the game, I was feeling overwhelmed and sorry for myself. She said that whenever you find yourself needing to make a choice on how to move something forward, don't ask "How will I ever get this done?" Ask yourself instead, "Who can I get to do this?" This gets back to the whole idea of being open to all possible resources and support. You really don't have to do it all yourself, nor should you. Effective business people and entrepreneurs know this.

From that day forward, when looking at all the choices I had that required a next step action, I would ask this powerful question. It has been a huge factor in helping me see many things through to fruition.

If you don't have time to move something forward and you honestly cannot take the time, then you should be opening up the possibility that someone else might be able to do a piece of it for you (and most likely that person could even do it better and get it done faster). The bottom line is that you have control over how it gets done even if you are not physically the one doing it. By letting go of a piece of it for someone else to put their energy behind it on your behalf, you are more in control than if it was still in your to-do pile with nothing progressing.

Something else to consider is when you have taken an idea or option as far as you can possibly take it, but now it is at a point or stage where it is out of your control. Perhaps you now must wait on someone else or a particular situation to occur before it can move forward. Instead of getting frustrated and impatient or dwelling on why it is taking so long (which drains your energy to focus on other things) step away from it, accept this temporary lull and put a system in place to check on its progress. Better yet, have someone else monitor it and follow up. Then put your energies around those options and choices which you do control to take the next step.

Sometimes stepping away for awhile can actually open up another avenue to explore. Coincidentally, I have even found that while working on an entirely different goal action item, I will come across another option to consider for the one that is in limbo. And then I no longer feel that there is only one choice and no need to wait for the situation that is out of my control. I like to say, if you think there is only one way to get to the next step or one choice in any given situation, then your eyes are wide shut. Even deciding to not make a move is making a choice, and sometimes is the very thing that needs to happen for another option to appear.

It's time to take a look at all those choices looming about in your to-do list and subconscious. Let's see what can be done to put them in motion.

EXERCISE 11:1

Do you have a lot of irons in the fire? Are there several things or projects you have started with none of them really progressing? List them and then answer these questions.

Look at the items on your list related to your business or work.

1. **Which of these current projects will most directly help you achieve your company's ultimate purpose?**

2. **Which of these projects will impact your bottom line with increased profit or greater sales or income to the business?**

3. **Which of these projects will help your business operate more effectively to free you or others up to focus on other things in the long term?**

4. **Which ones started out with gusto and then fizzled?** Why did this happen? Has something changed that now makes them not so appealing, or did something roadblock their progress?

5. **Which ones will have a direct impact in the most immediate way when completed?**

EXERCISE **11:1** CONTINUED

Look at the items on your list related to your personal life.

1. **Which ones will have a direct impact on the current personal goals you have identified as high priority?**

2. **Which of these current choices will most directly help you achieve your ultimate purpose?**

3. **Which ones are not related to your ultimate purpose but still need to be done because it is just part of life?**

4. **Which of these choices will ultimately free you or others to focus on other things in the long term?**

5. **Which ones started out with gusto and then fizzled?** Why did this happen? Has something changed that now makes them not so appealing or did something roadblock their progress?

EXERCISE 11:2

Are there things you know you need to get finished or to get started in order to take your enterprise or something in your life to the next level, but you cannot seem to find the time or focus to complete? List them here and answer these questions.

1. **What is the reason these things have not been started or progress has stopped?**

2. **What are the next phases needed to take it a step further?**

3. **Who or what could move them forward for you?**

"Our passion feeds our faith in ourselves and in what we are doing. When you are passionate about something, it is a part of you so completely that you simply believe. Call it blind faith; it is confidence in its purest sense.

Chapter 12
If Only I Had More Confidence

I am a collector of inspirations and insights. At the beginning of each month, I make it a practice to write a thought-provoking or motivational quotation for every day of that month in my appointment calendar. I have been doing this for years and it has proven to be a wonderful confidence booster. As a result of seeing a particular phrase on a particular day, I am often inspired or incited to action. This practice has also served as an excellent means of preparing me for the month ahead with an inspired mindset.

When it comes to insights, my most profound ones have been garnered through a continuous mode of learning by taking an honest and concentrated look at my mistakes and the mistakes others have made. It is through this intentional evaluation of how a problem, situation or decision could have been handled differently, adjusted, avoided or anticipated that discoveries are made and true growth occurs.

The greatest confidence builder for synergized entrepreneurs is the triumph involved in learning from mistakes, overcoming obstacles and being in a continuous state of personal and professional growth. But for others, these types of challenges can serve to diminish their confidence. Why is this?

In Chapter Six, I discussed how from the day we were born, our entire existence was built on learning from our mistakes. We attempted so many things, and might have triumphed only after multiple attempts. Yet we were not daunted. We simply kept at it because we did not have any reason or conditioning at the time to not continue to try, try again. Eventually, of course, we do get to an age where others' reasoning and opinions can have an impact on our confidence. In addition, as we get older, our simple triumphs are no longer enough to bring squeals of delight to those who raised us or witnessed various strides. The bar continually gets raised higher and, after a while, there will be times when we attempt something that we simply cannot accomplish. How we responded to these first non-achievements, and how we

Wallflower to Wall of Fame

When an introverted graphic designer decided to strike out on her own, she lacked confidence and felt unworthy. However, she was new to the area, found contentment in her creative side and wanted to pursue challenges that would keep feeding her creativity. A long-time mentor had helped her realize that to build self-confidence, she must build courage to step out of her comfort zone. She knew this is what she needed to do.

Her lack of confidence and comfort in crowds became painfully clear with her first efforts to attend events as a means of gaining business. The first event she attended, she found herself like the typical wallflower at a high school prom, hugging the wall, smiling nervously and looking away as others made connections and conducted business. During the second event, she ended up in tears and left early, physically feeling pain from the anxiety that the situation caused.

Her mentor advised, "If you cannot do something, act as if you can." Knowing that she needed to make a living, the freelancer was determined to make connections and get good business leads. So this time she went to the other extreme, because she thought this is what was expected by others. She became focused on what she wanted, which was business. She would speak about her design work and focus entirely on her own gain. She again came out of these networking events feeling frustrated and even worse, like she was a fake. She was not getting business and now she was not being herself either.

She finally had an epiphany when she took time to watch others whom she admired. The secret to their success was that they were more focused on helping others make connections, and in the process, they also reaped the benefit of making new connections. Once she realized it was not about her, but about others, there was a comfort in taking the focus away from her. She determined to become better at communicating and more comfortable conversing with people. She realized that part of growing and maturing was to find, learn and earn the tools to become the way she wanted to be instead of expecting it to magically manifest.

She found herself looking forward to networking opportunities because she could now put the focus on others and how she could help them. With this new and more comfortable approach came other opportunities to serve on boards or committees. Business started coming to her. She was no longer selling, but attracting business. She was a magnet and this in turn energized her confidence to step out even further.

As her business continued to grow, she gained the vision to focus on the niche of producing publications. Today her regional publications firm specializes in self-published books, magazines, catalogs, periodicals and marketing collateral, winning local, regional and national acclaim. In addition, this shy wallflower now speaks in front of audiences inspiring them with her message of hope, overcoming extreme odds and triumphing over them. She has won numerous awards for her business acumen and influence in her industry. All because she faced her fearful and wishful thinking head-on, and never looked back.

were encouraged or discouraged in these situations could very well have shaped our underlying confidence and our future approach to attempting new things.

I was blessed with a grandmother who reinforced that I could do anything if I put my mind to it. She inspired a will in me to always give anything that I wanted to do a try. She also instilled an understanding that if something did not work out, it happened for a very good reason. There is a saying that goes, "On the way to what I planned, something even better came along." Instead of fretting and feeling sorry for myself, it has been much more productive to be very aware and in tune with what might be just around the corner — that wonderful opportunity that could be missed if I was spending too much time sulking. My grandmother's wisdom has served me extremely well. I share it with you because, even if you did not have the blessing of someone like my grandmother, her sage advice can begin serving you well starting right now.

Confidence isn't about always getting everything right. Confidence is about being able to handle both success and failure undaunted, and then move on. It is also about understanding ourselves well enough to know what we are good at and where we might be limited in ability or understanding, so we can either find a way to compensate or accept our weaknesses and focus on our strengths.

One all too common way that your confidence can be undermined is by the company that you keep. As I mentioned, a quality that has served me well is an optimism to always look for the lesson or the opportunity rather than dwelling on the mistake or failure. What I quickly realized is that often any doubts I was feeling stemmed from allowing negativity to taint and affect my view — negativity from others who were probably not the best people to be in my circle of influence and support. One by one, over the course of years, I began to filter out those people who were continuous naysayers in both my personal and professional life, in order to allow my passion to thrive and survive.

Hope, faith and passion also play an important role in confidence. You wouldn't be where you are — in business for yourself — if you did not have a certain amount of hope, faith and passion in what you were doing. So what's stopping you now?

One of my favorite quotes reads, "Hope sees the invisible, feels the intangible, and achieves the impossible." Hope is also the one thing that can inspire alternatives when it seems that there is nothing you can do in a particular situation. Think about this for a moment and what it could mean for you and what it has meant for countless others. Hope is what dreams are made of. Dreams are what ideas are made of. Ideas are what our world is made of, resulting in some of the greatest innovations in our lives today.

Our faith comes from a variety of places. For some it is a spiritual or religious belief that there is a higher power helping to guide or assure us that we are safe and can trust in the future. For others, faith comes from what is tangible — overcoming challenges by our own tenacity and perseverance. Whatever gives you faith is right for you. What is important is to have it to keep you going in difficult times. And surround yourself with those whose faith can inspire or nurture your own.

Our passion feeds our faith in ourselves and in what we are doing. When you are passionate about something, it is a part of you so completely that you simply believe. Call it blind faith; it is confidence in its purest sense. Remembering what you are passionate about in your business and in your life and giving it your time will help re-ignite your faith and confidence in yourself.

EXERCISE 12:1

As you read this chapter, you may have already begun to get a clue about what may be undermining your confidence. However, answer these questions to further explore what could be affecting your confidence so that you can begin to overcome and reignite your hope, faith, passion, optimism and belief in who you are and what you are doing.

1. **Where do you lack confidence in what you are doing?** Where does this lack of confidence stem from? Make a list of all the reasons you believe you lack confidence. Now make a list of what you could do to overcome these feelings. Choose these ways listed to take action to overcome these feelings.

2. **Do the areas in which you lack confidence also coincide with areas that you simply are not passionate about?** If so, then why are you spending so much time in these areas? Is there someone else who could take this role so you can focus on where your passion lies? Is there training or some aspect of learning that you could gain that will help you build confidence if it is essential to your success?

3. **Take a look at your answers in Chapter Eight about your values and purpose.** How can these answers help you in evaluating your areas where you lack confidence? Are some of your values being challenged in a way that is undermining your efforts?

4. **List all the people in your life that you value or come into contact with on a daily basis.** Be totally honest and note how they are a positive influence or a negative one and why. Note also if they challenge you and if it is in a good way or a demeaning way. If there are those in regular contact with you who are highly negative or draining your confidence, how can you reduce or eliminate your interaction with them? Do they realize they are being negative and can this possibly be averted so they can become a positive influence?

5. **How are you inspired?** What can you begin to do on a daily basis to inspire you and build confidence in what you are trying to achieve where you lack confidence?

"Where we've gone astray is in thinking that money is the end all to achievement and success. As a result, we are too focused on making money because we equate it with the measure of our wealth. What it really takes is leveraging all of your resources."

Chapter 13
It Takes Money to Make Money, Unless You Don't Have It

The idea of capitalism has steered many of us into the wrong way of thinking. I'm not talking about free enterprise, as this is the exciting, sexy side of entrepreneurship. The reality is that we cannot do anything, or so we've been brought up to think, without money. There is not a day that goes by when money is not exchanging hands in order to acquire something we need, want or value. And money is a necessity for business to succeed. Of course it is. The problem lies in believing that money is the *only* resource that you have at your disposal.

Where we have gone astray is in thinking that money is the end all to achievement and success. As a result, we are too focused on making money because we equate it with the measure of our wealth. We have been lured into believing that it takes money to make money, so we get caught up in a cycle of making money to make more money. What it really takes is leveraging all of your resources. Savvy entrepreneurs recognize that wealth of resources is not just about money. Those who understand this concept end up creating their pot of gold and have fewer worries along the way. By thinking differently about your resources, you can stretch your money further, keep more money for yourself and give more money away.

So what are the other resources that are too often overlooked? In business and in life, you have a total of four resources at your disposal: time, people, technology and money. All should be considered and allocated to their best possible use and effectiveness. You should actually budget for each one of them at home and at work. The key to truly leveraging these resources is to consider how one can help you get more out of the other. Once you realize the powerful way you can put all of your resources to work, you will be witnessing the genius of synergy in motion.

HOME SWEET BUSINESS

The owner of a commercial videography company was sitting in his office as he talked with a marketing consultant about his goals for his company. As a certified scuba diver and a pilot, he had developed a niche in his business to handle unique video assignments from land, sea or air. He had been in business for more than two decades and he was looking toward semi-retirement and better leveraging his resources as a result. He wanted to shift his energies to working more from home. He already had a sophisticated editing suite built into his home, which he was using more and more instead of using the one at his high-end office space. The owner wanted to also step up his marketing efforts to specific niche opportunities.

As options were explored further, he was asked why he needed his expensive office space and how often clients actually came to the space versus him going to them. The shocking reality was that he was paying for an address that was draining his profits and not serving him from an image or a location standpoint. Once his lease, utilities and ancillary expenses were considered, thousands of dollars were literally not reaping the value associated with them.

With a dedicated editing suite already in place at home, easy modifications made the space a tax deduction as a home-based business. The swank office location was eliminated, which not only gave financial resources for the niche marketing, but also gave the owner peace of mind in using all of his resources wisely.

First, let's look at creative ways to get more for your money. Money can pose a barrier when determining a need to finance or purchase something that is substantial. We know this investment will help take the business to the next level, and yet the thought of outlaying "that kind of money" seems beyond comprehension. But again, we are so focused on the fact that it costs money that we are not thinking of any other resources we may be able to tap. We also tend to get stuck in an all-or-nothing frame of mind; as a result, aspects of the business get put on hold. It is important to know what something may cost in dollars. Then you need to open your mind to all possible resources and support that could help you acquire this business purchase in a manageable way. What about identifying someone seeking the same investment? Then you share the expense. A client and I shared an administrative employee for nearly two years. We each needed part-time help, but all the applicants were interested in full-time work. My client and I agreed on the benefits and shared all these expenses. This, of course, took some open-mindedness from the employee, but it worked perfectly.

Another aspect I see all too often is businesses not marketing because "it costs too much money." So many aspects of marketing are about leveraging people, time and technology, not just money. How can you share the marketing expense with another business going after the same market? How can you build a strong network outside of your customer base touting your business throughout the marketplace? How can you utilize technology and schedule windows of time to make marketing an everyday operational part of your business? Answer these questions and you have just exponentially increased your ability to be successful in marketing your business.

There is one final aspect of money that could help your business cash flow — bartering. I have been a member of a bartering service for more than a decade. I have leveraged this in phenomenal ways to gain equipment at a fraction of the cost of paying cash or to improve cash flow by receiving cash from the client for goods or services that were bartered through my business.

At first I wasn't sold on bartering. Why? Because I was doing it the way most business owners do, by trading services in a client-vendor relationship — in other words, swapping services or products. The problem with this is that one party often needs the other's services more. As a result, the other party may feel slighted with only one of them really getting what they needed, when they needed it. I had two different experiences where once my bartering partners got what they wanted, I was unable to receive my side of the deal. You can only imagine how soured I was on "doing it as a trade" after these instances.

A bartering service allows you to barter your services among an entire group. Therefore, you provide your services or products to one company and are able to choose from the entire network to gain what you need. As a result, my company has gained two copiers (including a high-resolution digital quality printer), catering, party talent, computers, printing services, gift certificates, and the list goes on. One of my most valued barters was booking a resort where a conference I was attending took place. It was part of the national barter network, so I was able to save on something I had budgeted for my business, and only had to pay the taxes on the room out-of-pocket.

Now that we have looked at how money is being spent, you need to take a look at all the ways your business is costing you and also take a look at how money in your personal life is flowing out. Then you need to think about what you can do with the other resources you have to make your money do more for you.

In looking at how your business is costing you, don't just look at the money that is being spent. What about the money that is not being made? One of the biggest pitfalls that start-up entrepreneurs fall into is not hiring when they should, so their time is spent on necessary, but non-income-generating activities. I have lost count of the number of times I have heard, "I should have hired her or him about a year or two ago." Typically an entrepreneur will wait until a critical point or a near breaking point of stress to hire that first employee or that first manager in their business. What is more important to notice, however, is the realization of two other resources — time and people — that were not being effectively leveraged. By hiring someone, the entrepreneur is able to better utilize time to generate more income — three resources working together versus one not working.

People are not just to be viewed as individuals you bring into your company on your payroll. People can also mean other companies and *their* people going to work for you … payroll, cleaning, bookkeeping, answering service, delivery, accounting, legal, marketing, training, IT support, and the list goes on. What tasks are you still doing in your business that you shouldn't be doing? What are your employees doing that is keeping them from income-generating activities?

Another aspect of an entrepreneur's time to consider relates to where they spend their time outside of the business under the guise of creating more business. The research my firm conducted in 2004 showed that high-growth entrepreneurs were strategically involved in two or three organizations on boards or committees. Want to guess how many organizations the stagnant or no-growth entrepreneurs were involved in? Whenever I ask this of a group I am speaking to, their answer is unanimously "zero." But this is actually not the case. Our research indicated that the no-growth business owners were involved in five or more organizations. They were literally volunteering their profits away. Clearly this was not a good strategic use of their time.

Because being involved in the right organizations in the right way is a valuable strategy for your business, let me help you make better choices. In any organization, whether it is civic, charitable, professional or trade, there are actually four levels of involvement: member, participant, involved, and strategically involved.

The first level is membership. As a member you may pay dues or decide to join in the group's purpose. You will likely receive information, regular communications and some ancillary benefits. But if you are doing nothing else, then you are merely a member.

The second level is being a participant. You receive communications and decide to attend functions or events that the group hosts. You meet and greet and most likely pass out several business cards in the process. But the reality is, this is still a very superficial involvement where acquaintances are made versus relationships being built. The best way to build relationships is to literally get involved.

The third level is being involved, but not necessarily in the most optimal way. Too many business owners don't take control of their involvements, but rather let the involvements take control of them. Here's the likely scenario. You become a member, start to participate in the organization, and then are approached and asked to be on a certain committee or the board. You say yes and it may be only later that you wonder what you got yourself into.

Here's what high-growth entrepreneurs do. They know exactly how they are going to be involved in an organization even before they pay their membership dues or decide to join the cause. This is the fourth and most desired level, which is being *strategically* involved. They have researched the opportunities in the organization where they can make a noticeable difference. They take control and get involved where they can best serve and where it will best serve their company in a win-win scenario. How do they gauge this? By considering these three things: 1) the group will put them in direct interaction with their ideal target customer; 2) the group will put them in direct interaction with those who would refer business to them; or 3) the group offers valuable access to resources or services that will help their business operationally.

High-growth entrepreneurs with employees also understand the value of getting employees strategically involved in the right organizations, resulting in spreading the

MIDNIGHT MADNESS

Sitting in an all-night quick-print service awaiting a client's fliers, a marketing firm owner was feeling total frustration. The client was originally going to print the fliers on her own from the file the marketing firm had created, but then could not find anyone to do it in the short time frame she had allowed. The owner received a call at 10:00 at night with the fliers needing to be ready for the event by 10:00 the next morning. By the time the owner retrieved the file from her office and got to the vendor, it was midnight. As she sat there waiting for the printing to be completed, she said to herself, "There has to be a better way."

Looking at all possible resources, she wondered if a high-quality digital printer was a possibility through the barter exchange in which her company was a member. She had accumulated quite a bit of barter credits and it did seem feasible. The next morning, the owner had her office manager inquire, and there was a company that could provide what the owner had in mind. A brand new digital printer could be purchased through the exchange for $12,500 worth of barter credit, plus out-of-pocket for barter fees and taxes at approximately $2000. But what did it really cost the marketing firm owner? With the out-of-pocket for payroll for the design and creative services provided to various barter network members, the printer actually cost the owner around $7,600, including the fees and taxes that had to be paid separately according to barter rules. This also allowed the firm to serve clients with fast short-run, high-quality printing and the ability to publish and produce its own materials entirely in-house, saving money and time.

wealth of the *people* resource for greater exposure of the company as a whole, versus being viewed as the only one that counts in the company.

As you can see, better use of people and better choices can capture a great deal of time for the entrepreneur and assure that the time is well spent. Time is an asset that is undervalued, even though everyone wishes they had more. I have devoted the entire next chapter to looking even more closely at time, so let's take a look at the other resource — technology.

You can either be a slave to technology or it can be a powerful operational and marketing support to your business. Once again, it is your choice. I discuss the time-wasting factors of technology in the next chapter, so let's focus on the aspect of technology as a time saver and business performer here.

I am completely sold on technology as a means of doing business. So are high-growth companies. These entrepreneurs know that technology is key to business operations. The Internet is also a critical success factor for these companies. They are using the Internet on a daily basis to communicate, conduct business or gain information and resources.

How can technology make your business better, serve your customers more effectively or make operations run more smoothly? After our entire office became networked, I realized the miracle of synchronizing and working with offline files. No more transferring back and forth on disks or flash drives. When I leave with my laptop, the files I work on away from the office automatically sync in the way I will be working with them. When I return, they automatically sync again. Remote access is the next step and has become a norm for many businesses. Our virtual society allows us to connect in a multitude of ways to conduct business wherever we are.

Most of this chapter has been dedicated to the business side of leveraging your resources. But you can use the same thinking to more effectively leverage the same four resources in your personal life as well. The same cleaning service that cleans your office may also clean your home at a discounted rate because you are already a customer. Families with vacation homes trade with others who have vacation homes in other locations — beach versus mountains versus golf resort versus a lake home. These places also can make great company retreat meeting spaces. See how opening up your mind to everything in life and work can help you become ingenious in your solutions?

Now it's time to help you begin to use all four valuable resources.

EXERCISE 13:1

So, what exactly are your attitudes about money that could be affecting your ability to identify or leverage other resources? Answer these questions to gain an understanding of how you view money as a whole. Chances are you have never really thought about this before, so it will be enlightening to discover why you approach money the way you do.

1. **When you hear the word money, what first comes to mind?**

2. **How did you view money growing up?** How was money depicted to you by your parents and family? Plentiful? Limited? Never Enough?

3. **Are you a saver or a spender?** Why?

4. **Where does money fall in your stress scale?** High? Low? Why?

5. **Are you a bargain shopper or do you buy only the best, with money being no object?** Or are you somewhere in between? Why do you think you are this way?

6. **What is your idea of a good value for your money?** What is your idea of wasting money?

7. **Who do you admire in how they handle money and why?**

EXERCISE 13:2

Now it is time to help you get beyond money being your only answer. Here are some questions to help you open your mind to other resources you can tap into:

In your business:

1. **Is there money not being made because you or others are being pulled away from income-generating activity?** Take a look at these non-income activities and brainstorm on ways for these tasks to be done using technology or other people.

2. **How could technology help you serve customers better, operate more efficiently, simplify a function, or elevate a service or product offering for competitive advantage?**

3. **What are you doing internally that may be better served by outsourcing it to other people?**

4. **How can you better use your people's time to engage them in the marketing side of operations?**

5. **What are some needs in your business that seem out of reach at the moment?** Could they be attainable through bartering or sharing with someone?

In your life:

1. **How can you leverage the time of others in your household to gain more time for yourself?**

2. **Where can technology be used to simplify your life at home?**

3. **Who can you share expenses or services with to gain a better rate?**

4. **Who can you potentially trade services with such as house sitting, lawn care or babysitting to gain more money for other things or more time for yourself?** Remember that it does not have to be the same service.

"Your time is no more valuable than anyone else's. It is only valuable to you. You have the same amount of time in a day as everyone else does, so it is clearly how you use it and how you leverage every moment that counts."

Chapter 14
Making Time Your Greatest Asset

In 1995, I was sitting in my office feeling overwhelmed and frustrated by all that needed to be done. Out of this exasperation, I proclaimed, "Oh, if only I had more time!" Sitting across from me at her desk in our one room office was my administrative dynamo, Ann Lampron. She has become a friend and someone I admire greatly. And this particular moment clinched that respect for a lifetime, when she said without blinking an eye, "You have the same amount of time as everyone else does. It is just a matter of how you use it."

My first reaction was total annoyance, as this was not the answer I wanted to hear. I wanted a pep talk. I wanted an "Oh, you can handle it, Sherré." But she was totally right and at that very moment, I got it. Her "slap-in-the-face" dose of reality was exactly what I needed to hear. And I remind myself of this every time I start to feel time getting away from me. As a result, time is no longer my enemy, but my true ally in whatever I do. It can be that way for you too. It is all a matter if how you use time and how you leverage every moment.

I know, this sounds like more pressure, doesn't it? Not at all. You just have to start thinking of time in a different frame of mind. Time is the one resource that you always have available to you every minute of every day. We all have the same amount given to us, as my friend so blatantly reminded me. Think about this for a moment. Is there any other resource you have that is available to you without exception? The key is to view time as a valued resource.

Part of the main reason that time becomes our enemy is that we allow everyone else to dictate how and when we use it. Time can only become your ally and greatest asset once you take control of how your time is used. So you need to consider how you are allocating your time, just like you allocate other assets in your business and life. I call it taking a time inventory assessment.

The first thing you need to take inventory of is everything that you believe wastes

Class Act

An owner of a high-end gourmet cooking boutique also offered small hands-on cooking classes for 8-12 people, taught by experienced chefs. These classes were a huge hit, resulting in a demand to double the class schedule. The boutique was inundated with inquiries and classes became booked nearly two months in advance. The challenge was that everything — from processing payments to confirming registrations — was being handled manually by the owner. She usually worked on these tasks late at night and on weekends because of the retail-hour demands. Finally, the owner realized that technology was the answer. Her retail website was programmed with online registration, online payment, automated responses and reminders.

She also got her chefs more involved in the corporate events she was undertaking and paid them a fee, while still making a nice profit for her business. The result was that she was able to effectively double her class offerings and corporate offerings, plus get her life back to enjoy personal pursuits in her retail off-hours.

or steals away your time. Is it looking for things or trying to remember something? Being stuck in traffic? Traveling for business? Email? Talking on the phone? Playing phone tag? People just dropping in? Meetings?

If you find yourself frustrated by looking for things, I have one very critical piece of advice. Get organized. Have a particular place for everything and then do not deviate. From how your desk and office is set up, to how you retrieve or lay down things as you walk in, out and through your home, you will recapture amazing amounts of time simply by putting things in order and keeping them that way. And if you can't do it, get someone to help you, and then hold yourself and everyone else accountable. It is time and money well spent.

If you find yourself forgetting things on a regular basis, then carry a small pocket notebook that never leaves your side to write each thing down as soon as you think of it. This has been an amazing tool for me. The minute I think of anything that requires action or something I simply want to be assured I don't forget, I write it in my little notebook. And I have learned never to trust my own belief that I will remember a certain thought or idea later on. I write it down. Period. And I always write it down in that same little notebook, not a sticky note or scrap piece of paper that is easily misplaced. We certainly don't want you forgetting something and then not being able to find that piece of paper that has on it what you forgot.

Traveling for business or being stuck in traffic are the time wasters that I often hear about. Personally, I used to despise traffic so much that I would get myself in a state of mind that actually perpetuated the problem. First, you simply have to accept that until we can teleport ourselves like Captain Kirk on Star Trek, driving or flying is how we get from point A to point B. Accepting this as a part of business and life is the reality. However, this does not mean you cannot make the most of it. Savvy entrepreneurs know how to make the most of these types of situations. You will see them reading on the airplane and working on their laptop or returning phone calls while waiting to board. If traveling for business involves a car, then you are back to the same scenario as the person stuck in traffic. Listening to audio books, dictating your thoughts into a recorder or preparing for your next meeting in your mind can be a wonderful use of the time. The key is to view these windows of time as opportunities to accomplish something else. When I changed my mindset about traffic and just accepted it, not only did I recapture time for learning through audio books and preparatory thinking, but I also reduced my stress level.

As for emails and meetings, these are totally within your power to control. Don't become a slave to your email. It is easy to do and eats into many entrepreneurs' days

LEGAL EASE

An attorney in a solo practice felt like she had reached her billable capacity and was frustrated by this realization. The quandary was that she was billing about 40 percent of her time, yet putting in 60+ hours. She had plans to start a family and her desire to reduce the hours she worked and increase the income she generated was creating stress that seemed to have no solution. A consultant suggested hiring an office assistant for at least ten hours a week. She was reluctant at first, seeing only the cost versus the opportunity for her to focus on more billable work in fewer hours. She tried it on a subcontractor basis and within two months, the subcontractor was working nearly 25 hours-per-week. Not only was the assistant doing office work, but also marketing and research support. The research support could be billed at three times what was being paid to the assistant, which more than paid for her fees.

Shortly thereafter, the lawyer found out she and her husband were expecting twins. Her assistant continued to serve clients' needs during the lawyer's maternity leave. Today this attorney enjoys a higher level of billable hours-per-week, a more controlled work schedule to enjoy her new family, and enough support so that her time is spent where it is most needed.

because you react like Pavlov's dog whenever that "You've got mail" tone sounds off. Dedicate certain times of the day to check your email and stick to it. Turn the tone sound off and concentrate on your work. If there is a particular email that you are expecting, ask the person to call you or text message you when it is sent, so you know to look for it instead of constantly checking and then getting distracted by other emails that could wait for a response. Let technology work for you by using the security devices that filter spam messages. Organize your important emails into folders so they are easier to find later, and delete those that are of no value or relevance.

When it comes to meetings, I have found more and more entrepreneurs allotting certain days for meetings and certain days for in-office work. Determining if a meeting can be just as easily conducted by telephone eliminates travel and chit-chat time. Telephone meetings are always more efficient. Of course, there will be times when face-to-face meetings are required, but conducting at least some of your meetings by phone saves time and money.

The telephone is another device that is blamed for eating into time. Just as you set time for meetings and in-office work, schedule time for making calls and returning calls. And please, when returning calls, leave a detailed message so specific action can be taken when the call is returned or better still, does not have to be returned. Phone tag can be avoided by simply leaving a complete message after the beep, including when you can be reached or what action needs to be taken by the other party without a need to call back.

The next thing to assess in your time usage inventory is anything that takes you away from what you would really like to be doing. Are there obligations you no longer want to participate in? Are there things you are doing that someone else could or should be doing instead? Some of the exercises in this chapter and others will help you think through these and gain some perspective on how you might reallocate or eliminate some of these unwanted commitments.

The third and final consideration is activities dictated by others that affect the use of your time. What does this mean for you? Children's or family activities? Business events? Business trade or professional meetings? Client or customer meetings? Use the exercises in this chapter to help you fully disclose all of these, so you can more effectively deal with them as you view your time in this new way.

Now, look at your time in the span of an entire week or month. Are meetings scattered here, there and everywhere? Are you trying to fit time to do in-office work or fieldwork around these meetings? Are you traveling from one end of the spectrum and back, dictated by others' preferences versus your convenience? Well, no wonder you feel like you cannot get anything done!

A mistake that some people make is believing that their time is more valuable than others. When this occurs, you immediately place yourself in a mindset of entitlement and competing for time versus collaborating and cooperating to gain better use of your time through the assistance of others. The key to effectively leveraging other people's time is to align yourself with those who also consider time to be a valuable and respected resource. This will assure that your time is being respected and valued. What is important to remember here is that your time is no more valuable than anyone else's. It is only valuable and precious to you. I intentionally seek out doctor's offices and healthcare practices that guarantee you are in and out within a certain timeframe. If a client or vendor does not share a mutual respect for time, then they should no longer be a client or vendor.

The ultimate benefit in conducting this comprehensive time inventory assessment is that you will find ways to recapture some much needed and desired free time for yourself. And this is the most precious time of all.

EXERCISE 14:1

How could you use your time in a way that makes it an asset and something you truly cherish versus something that plagues you? Answer these questions and see how you can shift your thinking and ways of doing things to help you do a time inventory assessment and better leverage your time as one of your greatest assets:

1. **How do you control how your time is spent?** Are you doing anything that is eating away at your time on a regular basis that you wish you did not have to do?

2. **What is taking time away from what you really want to be doing?** What are you a slave to that distracts you from what you want to be spending your time doing?

3. **Where do you believe your time is best spent?**

4. **What do you consider to be time wasters?** Are some of these enjoyable? Why do you feel they are time wasters?

5. **Of those time wasters that are not enjoyable, what can you do to avoid them?** Is there someone else that can do them? Is there another way you can approach the situation to recapture some of your time?

6. **How do you protect your time?** Are you taking the initiative to offer options for your schedule or are you allowing yourself to be at the mercy of everyone else's time?

7. **Who in your work or life does not appear to value your time?** Can you identify why your time is viewed as not as valuable in their eyes and why?

8. **If someone in your life or business does not value your time or takes it for granted, can this be directly addressed and new expectations set?**

"Your passion is why you are in business for yourself and what gets your juices flowing for whatever you set out to do. It's also what stirs such emotion in you that it can frustrate instead of invigorate you, especially if the right support is not there when you need it."

Chapter 15
Gaining Support in Life and Work

Do you awaken each day looking forward to what lies ahead, or do you dread interacting with those around you? Do you end each day excited about what the next day will bring, or are you still replaying the day and some of the frustrations that seemed to pull you away from where you really wanted to be focusing?

When the passion for what you are doing is waning, you may need to take a look around you. There is nothing more draining than feeling like you are in it alone. It creates the potential for a reversal in fortunes. The reality is that as much as we profess great pride in our pioneering ways as entrepreneurs, by human nature, it is much more rewarding to have others along to enjoy the ride. And having others by our side makes reaching the destination even better than we could have imagined.

Passion can be a double-edged sword. On one side, it is why you are in business for yourself. It's what gets your juices flowing for whatever you set out to do. It is also what stirs such emotion in you that it can frustrate instead of invigorate you, especially if the right support is not there when you need it. For some entrepreneurs, this can be paralyzing. This is also the point at which they might downsize or give up on their dream altogether. What a shame. When all they had to do was be open to all possible support and resources.

One of the most profound ways I see entrepreneurs sabotaging themselves is by not sharing or involving anyone in what they envision. Are you one of these entrepreneurs? Could you be alienating support that is right before your eyes and under your nose? Have you shared your passion, your vision and your mission, and what these might mean for the business and its marketplace?

If you don't want to feel alone in your journey, then don't be alone. Start enabling those around to be a part of the exciting ride. But it is not enough to simply recite your mission statement — you must somehow make them a part of the excitement. Don't just tell them. Inspire them with your vision. Let them feel your passion. Allow them to embrace the

From MRIs to Artist's Eye

The idea of being in his own business or following his love of photography was not even a remote consideration for a long-time MRI technologist and department supervisor. He considered his photography hobby a form of stress relief and a means of escape, as were his mountain biking and volunteer work building bike and hiking trails in a local state park. However, he eventually realized the life-changing power of emotional support and inspiration. For him, it came in the form of someone in his life who saw his talent as something that could be more than a hobby.

He met his entrepreneur wife online and within one year they were married. As they hiked together, he would whip out his camera and capture shots along the way. One outing took them to a botanical park. His wife encouraged him to submit his images to the photo contest the park was sponsoring, and he won his first award. Her encouragement did not stop there, as she introduced him to her business world, and before long he was getting photography assignments for commercial work, family portraiture and magazine shoots. He also helped architectural and residential design clients win awards for their work through the stunning imagery he captured on film.

He was enjoying a new career in photography that would soon allow him to leave the healthcare world behind, but his love of nature and what the sensitive eye can see was still at the heart of his passion for photography. At the publishing of this book, an entire line of wearable, inspirational and decorative products featuring his abstract nature photography was launched. A portion of the proceeds go toward not-for-profits dedicated to sustainable living and creating a greener world.

possibilities right along with you. Let them know the challenges ahead and invite them to help you overcome these obstacles. I am not just talking about employees either. Anyone who interfaces with your business could be a conduit of support by inspiring support from a growing number of others. All you have to do is let them in. It is really that simple.

If you have ever lamented in exasperation that your employees "don't have a clue," ask yourself if *you* may be to blame. Could your employees really not have a clue *or* could it be that you haven't allowed them the pleasure of knowing and truly understanding what you are up to in the first place? If you operate your business in a vacuum you are sucking in air and nothing else. If you operate your business like an incubator, you are nurturing and growing it with everyone warmed to its possibilities, and nurturing it right along with you.

Suppose you have clearly shared your vision and the future you see, and there are those that still don't get it? If you can honestly confirm that you have kept them completely informed, then it may be that those who seemed to buy in at one time no longer get it now that the company has evolved. It may be time for them to move on. This can be especially tough when an employee has been with you for a long period of time. In these cases, the more honest you are, the more positively this situation can be resolved.

Now this doesn't mean that you want to get rid of everyone in your company that may challenge what you are doing. You do not want a bunch of "yes people" around you either. Being challenged to make sure that you have thought through all aspects of a new initiative is a highly positive, desirable and downright stimulating part of taking the venture to another level. I enjoy a wonderful circle of advisors, friends, employees and colleagues who challenge me to take my thinking to a higher level or bring an idea to its greatest potential. The difference here is that there is a mutual respect; they desire to see the company succeed and I want to see those involved with me succeed. They are not pointing out oversights or trying to find things wrong to make sport of it, but are genuinely considering all options and viewpoints to make a good idea become a great one.

Another aspect of support is the equity that others bring to your business. Most business owners think of equity in assets and what the business is worth. But what about sweat equity and the emotional equity in your business? Sweat equity is something you are all too familiar with — this is likely how you got your business off the ground. Additional support and assistance for your business from someone else can also be in the form of sweat equity.

Emotional equity means that you are no longer in this venture alone and it has a powerful role in inspiring you to achieve your goals and overcome obstacles. I spoke a little about this in the chapter on confidence. The company that you keep is an aspect of support on the emotional side that cannot be overlooked or underestimated in regard to

Sweat and Cheers

A sole operator of a custom cabinetry business was burning the candle at both ends and it was beginning to take a toll on his business and his health. His services were in demand and his business had a strong reputation for the quality products he produced. But he was having a hard time keeping up with the ordering, specifying, estimating and scheduling of installation crews. He secretly wished for a clone. As with most entrepreneurs, he was also having a hard time with the idea of adding someone to his payroll. He worried about the pressure of having a full-time employee who needed to be the family breadwinner. He shared his frustration with a colleague in the industry who just so happened to be looking for a way to leave the corporate environment and acquire something that he could consider his own.

Within months, they had determined a mutually agreeable arrangement. The owner's new partner would come on and work a portion of his equity in the business as sweat equity, while also putting some dollars into the business for capital influx. Having someone on board with the experience to manage the details of the business enabled the owner to focus on his vision and keeping clients happy. The business prospered and expanded, and both partners realized more satisfying personal lives as well.

the impact it has on your ability to succeed.

A circle of influence and support within and outside of your business and your life is part of how this emotional equity gets built. You should surround your business and life with those who are champions, cheerleaders, confidants and constructive critics. You never know where support may come from until you open yourself up and welcome it — through engaging people in what you are trying to do, sharing your vision and communicating the kind of support you need to succeed. This circle of influence and support widens the spectrum of options available to you regarding each new challenge or initiative. You are no longer doing all the thinking. Others are engaged and a part of the solution too, sometimes working on your behalf when you least expect it.

How can you attract more support for your business outside of your business? The best and most sincere way is by practicing a mindset of offering support to others. Being open to all possible support and resources means being open to giving support and being a resource. Actions most certainly speak louder than words. Do your actions encourage support or discourage it? The saying "what goes around comes around" is one to be taken seriously. In the research we conducted, high-growth companies understood the merits and value of giving back to the community in both small and big ways. These companies made charitable and civic involvements an aspect of their business as part of their strategic plan for success — not to make them look good, but because it made them feel good in return for the good fortune they had received.

Additionally, offering help to others in small ways can bring big opportunities to you when least expected. I have always considered it good stewardship on both a personal and professional level to help whenever possible. A local group was putting together a fundraising event for a local YMCA that was in the capital building stages. My company was approached to do a printed program associated with the fundraising event. We offered our graphics support and reduced printing costs to help the group out. The contacts made from this small gesture have resulted in numerous resources and support coming to me and my business.

Attitude is everything when it comes to attracting the type of support you need for your business. If you totally and utterly believe in what you are doing and are passionate in a positive, uplifting way, you will inspire and engage others. Your attitude will be contagious. Others will see you take action, and before you know it, all kinds of initiatives will take place on your behalf, bringing your goals closer to realization.

EXERCISE 15:1

In order to gain the support you feel is missing, you must take a look at where support is lacking or counterproductive to your ultimate plan.

1. **Who in your life is not supportive or simply does not seem to "get" what you are trying to achieve?** Before you decide to eliminate them from your life, especially if they are a key part of your life like a spouse or family member, answer the following questions:

   a. Are you supporting what they do? Are you engaged in what they do?

   b. When is the last time you sat down and really shared what you are trying to accomplish and what they could do to help support you?

   c. Is there a common factor that could come into play that could bring you together in a mutually beneficial way?

   d. Have you identified and expressed ways in which achieving your goals can compliment them achieving their goals?

   e. Have they always been negative or unsupportive or has this occurred only in respect to one particular issue or incident? If one of the latter, what is the underlying reason, and can it be resolved?

2. Take a look at each goal that is getting nowhere or not progressing as effectively as you would like. Answer these questions to identify how you can rally more support.

a. Does your goal require input from a variety of perspectives? Could an advisory council serve a purpose in achieving the goal?

b. Can you segment the goal into manageable pieces so that those who support you can take ownership of its progress to help you move it forward?

c. List the type of support needed for each goal and who is directly affected by the goal. Can these individuals contribute in some way? Do they know other resources you could tap into for support?

"Failure is an illusion. Everything you do produces a result. Some results were what you desired and some did not turn out exactly as you had hoped. This doesn't mean you failed."

Chapter 16
Failure is Not an F Word

I grew up in a hard-working, blue collar family in a multi-generation farming community where it was expected that you would carry on like everyone else. To be a dreamer and someone who had ideas outside of this way of life was considered unrealistic, downright rebellious and a formula for failure. So early in my life, I was hearing messages about failure and witnessing people whose fear of failure kept them right where they were. It can be so much easier to just go with the flow and carry on with the way things have always been, versus stepping outside that comfort zone. I have many wonderful memories of growing up and am proud of where I come from, but I still had something deep inside me that wanted to explore beyond those boundaries — to be all that I knew I could be. For a lot of people, going with the flow is actually how they are happiest and exactly what they want to do. I admire anyone who is doing exactly what he or she desires.

But what about the rest of us, who thrive on being challenged and stepping outside of our comfort zones? Well, for one thing, that is why we are entrepreneurs. Remember the thrill of starting your business? Remember how you were scared beyond imagination and yet, there was nothing that was going to stop you? Keep remembering this. You need to bring it back on your radar as you venture into the realm of synergizing your life.

I realized my fear of failure was actually one of the culprits holding me back from realizing what I could ultimately do. I'd find myself thinking back to my childhood years and recalling, "Maybe this will be the time when it all comes crashing down." As optimistic as I thought I was, I still found myself with an alternate doomsday scenario running through my head. This is why I decided that asking myself "What if…?" was not the right approach. At first, the "what if" thinking explored my dreams and vision of potentially exciting things. However, it also would lead to the "what if" thinking on the flip side and convince me not to move forward, at least not right

SEEING THROUGH THE SPOILAGE

A Japanese immigrant turned serial entrepreneur never forgot his roots and the wise teachings of his mother: "When a business don't work … then you got to know to walk away."

This valuable advice came to the forefront when this successful entrepreneur found himself in a geoduck debacle. His Japanese-inspired ventures included martial arts training and Asian sauce production, which attracted him to investing in the harvesting and distribution of geoducks, large clams used as a base for many sushi recipes. At first, the company showed great promise as an importer of the product from his native country. However, problems started to arise as more and more shipments arrived spoiled. Then a tragedy occurred when a diver harvesting geoducks was killed in an accident. A believer in karma, the entrepreneur determined the risks were too great to continue. He decided to close the business.

Always one to allow a so-called failure to be a learning experience, he studied all aspects of the enterprise and what went wrong. In reviewing the quandary of the spoiled shipments, he discovered a true opportunity existed in developing a company focused entirely on shipping perishable products overseas. His next serial success was born, evolving into a global freight-forwarding business that expanded from perishables to shipping non-perishable products for customers such as Nike.

then, but maybe later. "What if" thinking causes you to make decisions based on conjecture and worries versus reality and what you can and cannot control. The result is procrastination. I wouldn't totally let go of a particular desire, only determine that perhaps now was not the time. I wasn't ready. If I waited, I would have a greater chance of success. Sound familiar?

The idea of failure is conceived in our own minds, based primarily on beliefs or other people's expectations. Think about it. Is what you fear about failure actually the result of what others think failure is? If so, it is a waste of your time. Failure is an illusion. Everything you do produces a result. Some results were what you desired and some were not. That doesn't mean you failed. It simply means you need to try a different approach or make a different choice next time.

The shame of it all is when people just stop trying because of their fear of failure. If you cannot achieve success in the first few attempts, then you stop. One example is vying for awards and accolades for your business. Something that I have witnessed time and time again is an entrepreneur making it into a coveted finalist position in a Business Owner of the Year or Entrepreneur of the Year Award event. Instead of enjoying the achievement at this level, having made the cut among hundreds considered, they are stressed about "what if" they don't win. So, what if they don't? Here they are, being recognized as the cream of the crop in business, and all they can think about is not winning. Worse yet, they think if they don't win, then that's it, they are done and they won't waste their time again.

I simply do not understand this failure-focused way of thinking, especially during a time when their success is being recognized. You are reading a book written by the Susan Lucci of entrepreneur awards. I have won awards in my business on a local, state, regional, national and international basis. However, in my area's coveted Entrepreneur of the Year Award, I have been a finalist multiple times without winning. I consider this a huge honor, not a curse. Do you hear the optimism in what I write here?

Part of the reason I have this optimism is a result of an exercise I take myself through whenever I weigh a risk. I have identified four questions to ask myself as better alternatives to the "what if" question. I have posed these same questions to clients and those struggling with the fears of failure, venturing into unexplored territory or going outside their comfort zones. These questions are: Why? Why not? Why not me or my business? and Why not now? They force you to look at the reality and what is really holding you back. This validates that you actually have nothing to fear, as the saying goes, but fear itself.

Not Being Floored by the Odds

In the 1980s, the tile manufacturing industry was beginning to realize extensive overseas competition and consolidation, resulting in smaller custom tile manufacturers feeling the squeeze. Competitive overseas pricing was causing sales to drop and margins to fall for these small tile manufacturers. As a result, a family-owned company that manufactured handmade tiles was having a problem gaining sales for its products, which were at a much higher price point than competitors. After investigating all possible ways to cut costs in operations without sacrificing the unique custom appeal of the tile, the company realized it simply could not compete on price. Numerous other tile manufacturers were going out of business trying to compete on price, and the family did not want to be another casualty.

Out of fear from what they witnessed happening to others came a determination to succeed where others had failed. The family hired a marketing firm to identify how they could better compete within a price sensitive market. The key, they quickly learned, was to redirect their focus away from the market that was price sensitive — the builder — to the market that was looking for and desiring unique and distinctive flooring and walls — the architect, designer and high-end custom homeowner.

Other tile companies were simply showing their tile as products in a catalog, emphasizing price; but the custom tile company presented its tile in unique and appealing end applications, inspiring creativity and ideas in architects, designers and homeowners. In addition, the company prepared a special marketing piece that showcased the signature way each tile was marked with pride by the "hands that made it." This piece allowed distributors to better understand the higher price and bring the unique product line to the attention of architects and designers.

While even more tile companies have gone by the wayside as a result of automated processes and subsidized imports, this handmade tile company has grown to be America's largest manufacturer of handmade ceramic tile.

So how did this affect my attitude toward being a finalist yet again in the entrepreneur award? It has made my conviction to persevere even stronger. The funny thing is that after the last time of not winning, people approached me, saying that they did not understand why I did not win and why the one chosen did. Because I had already gone through my "why not" scenario, I could answer it quite easily. After all, every company represented in the competition was a phenomenal choice. I had my own favorite if I did not win, and that happened to be the company that did win. I cheered as loud as everyone when the winner's name was called. So when asked, I simply answered with the reason why that company deserved to win, with a smile and total confidence.

Do you have a failure driven attitude? Or do you have an attitude that empowers you to see the opportunities even when things don't go according to plan? Remember that optimism empowers your spirit and pessimism devours your spirit. Don't let pessimism, especially imposed by others, devour yours.

EXERCISE 16:1

Make a list of goal-related activities that you procrastinate about, keeping you from taking the next step toward your goal. Also make a list of things you have attempted to do and did not work out as planned. Then ask yourself these questions:

1. **Why?** Why should I go for it or go for it again? Why is this important to me?

2. **Why Not?** What is holding me back or could pose an obstacle? How could I overcome any obstacle? Why do I deserve to achieve this?

3. **Why Not Me?** What about me specifically could be a reason that I would succeed? What about me could cause me not to succeed? What are ways I could overcome this fear and succeed?

4. **Why Not Now?** Why is now a good time? What could make this not be a good time and why? What resources or support could I tap into to make this the right time?

EXERCISE 16:2

Answering the "why" and the "why not" questions forces you to look at reality — your reality — versus imagined factors. What it also does is help you take an honest look at each reason you cite and objectively refute or validate it. You will be putting the reasons to move forward with an idea and the reasons that are holding you back side by side. Then you move on to the "why not me" and "why not now" questions. These often help you put things into even clearer perspective as you explore your answers.

Next to all the reasons "not," note what is in your control, could be in your control, and what is outside of your control. Focus on those things that are within your control. Then stop procrastinating and put these things into action. Pretty soon, you too will have a much different view on failure. I guarantee it.

"Success can only become tangible once you define what it means to you and only you. The reality is that we have small successes every day and if leveraged properly, they add up to our ultimate success, created and determined from the inside out."

Chapter 17
Success Your Way, Every Day

Ahhh ... the ambiguity of success. It is something that we all strive to have, and yet no two people would define it in exactly the same way. For some, it is all about the money being made or in one's possession. For others, it is being recognized and honored. For some, it is competing and winning on a variety of fronts. For others, it is simply being happy, loved, content and fulfilled on a day-to-day basis. What is it for you?

Success is an intangible. It means many things to many people because we all come from different viewpoints and experiences that shape our idea of what success is and is not. We don't formulate our concept of success in a vacuum. We first look at success through the eyes of others. Our parents. Our teachers. Our coaches. Our friends. All have played a role in shaping the concept of success in our minds.

As we get older, we get caught up in the trappings of others' perceptions of success, hence making success seem unobtainable or even undesirable. We see how someone else has achieved success and we think we cannot possibly live up to that standard or by comparison, we have what it takes. We may even find our perception of success being based on those we don't necessarily admire. If we don't like their conduct or how they use their success, we use it as an excuse for not wanting success ourselves.

I have fallen into both of these success traps. The first trap presented itself to me as a child. Growing up with kids that seemed to have everything handed to them as a result of their parents' money, suggested to me that money had something to do with success. These kids seemed charmed and therefore, could do nothing wrong and got whatever they wanted or set out to achieve. Fortunately for me, this was not a deterrent. While I saw a connection between money and success, I did not believe you needed to have money to be successful. I believed that my success would lead me to the money I needed to live comfortably.

The second trap involves not wanting to be like those who have become successful.

AUTHENTIC SUCCESS

A regional director of an IT consulting firm led the company to record sales and award-winning recognition, building her division from six to seventy-six consultants within an eighteen-month period. The emotional high from managing and leading the process inspired her to consider starting her own IT consulting firm, but she held off due to the comfort of her current position and a slight fear of not having a big company with its resources behind her.

However, when Y2K hit the marketplace, she began to see a side of her industry she did not like — greed. The entire conversion premise associated with Y2K became highly lucrative to the point that many companies were taking advantage of the situation by over-charging clients, padding expenses and engaging in other dishonest practices.

In August of 2000, she set out on her own, determined to prove that a business could make a profit and serve the client's best interests with good old-fashioned values. She took a leap of faith almost immediately after starting her business by negotiating a sublease in a downtown high rise building, so she could be in the heart of where successful companies were located. Her authentic approach to business paid off. Her company turned a profit its first quarter and into its first year, which was unheard of in the industry.

Then the dot-com bubble burst, followed shortly by 9-11, and the large public companies that were the core of her business began cancelling or delaying contracts. She was seeing projected sales about to go spiraling downward if she didn't make some critical decisions and consider her options. She was able to quickly repackage her company's offerings for markets still doing business during this economic downturn. She established three business divisions focused on government work, small business IT support and quality process improvements for large companies. During the time between 2002 and 2004, when more than half of her competitors had gone out of business, her company's revenue doubled.

But the challenges did not stop here. At this same time she was diagnosed with a condition called palindromic rheumatism, which later evolved into rheumatoid arthritis. She experienced unpredictable attacks on various joints which would incapacitate her for days. During this period, she considered it a successful day if she made it to the office and through the day. She hired a key manager, a professional she had groomed at a previous company, to help her run the business as she coped with this volatile illness.

Through a variety of treatments, holistic and medical, she was able to gain control and get back to a point where she could once again work effectively on a full time basis. However, it was then that she started to really examine what was important to her and what her true purpose was in her life and work. Working with a life coach, she had two pivotal realizations. She believed her health needed to take precedence over anything else in order to truly enjoy her life moving forward. This meant that this self-proclaimed workaholic was no longer going to feel guilty about not going into work. She also determined that where she gained great joy at work was in mentoring other women and helping them advance in their careers. She wanted to inspire other women by what she had learned in growing her company while revisiting her life.

She resolved to enjoy all aspects of her life, health, work and family. She now spends more time with her three grandchildren, children and husband. She has become involved in a variety of industry and community endeavors as a means of giving back, and she continues to strategically move the company forward while enjoying her life and health.

In spite of all the challenges, this entrepreneur and her team were able to maintain a profit every quarter since inception. Her company has been recognized for her efforts to mentor women in the IT field on a local, regional and national level, as a top enterprising woman-owned company and an Inc. 5000 company. The company's impressive growth, of more than 200 percent on average each year over a five-year period, was recognized on a national level, with the company being ranked #10 in Harvard University's Top 100 Initiative for a Competitive Inner City Award in 2008.

Key to her success was being able to redefine success on her terms every step of the way.

This was a huge one for me. Into my twenties, I met numerous people that thought their success gave them the right to mistreat people, disrespect courtesies, abuse the system and engage in other behaviors that did not reflect my values. This made achieving success seem unappealing to me. My observations of these numerous people told me that success seemed to change people for the worse instead of for the better.

I have witnessed how the fear of success resulted in individuals abusing themselves with addictions and behaviors that sabotaged their success. They reached a level of accomplishment that they perhaps felt they did not really deserve, so they subconsciously put themselves on a path that would guarantee their success was short-lived.

The key to getting over your fear of success is to stop basing your idea of it on someone else's success — good, bad or otherwise. This requires an evolution to release the negative side of success. Instead, acknowledge and appreciate in others the positive and desired side of success. You can then determine your own definition of success and begin to work toward it. You are creating a success filter customized to your beliefs and values, not someone else's. This is why identifying your values, mission and vision is an important exercise in Chapter Eight.

Instead of looking at people whose success has made them unappealing, look for examples of those who share and live your values. These success mentors and role models are those of your own choosing, not those who have been imposed upon you. There is a difference, and once you really start evaluating what success means to you from a basis of your values, then you will see the difference.

Once you understand the difference, it is perfectly fine to be inspired by others' successes. Just don't be focused on attempting to mimic their success. When you try to duplicate their good fortune, you are placing yourself in a competitive mindset. You are no longer doing it for yourself, but rather to prove yourself against another. Save your competitive spirit for excelling in customer service and devising strategies in your marketplace. Create your own version of success and only compete with yourself to achieve it.

Success can only become tangible once you define what it means to you and only you. The reality is that we have small successes every day and if leveraged properly, they add up to our ultimate success, created and determined from the inside out. The first and only real way to get a handle on success is to understand what it looks like and feels like for you … and only you.

EXERCISE 17:1

First, let's take a look at your current perception of success to see if we can help you shift it in a more positive, effective direction. Answer these questions to gain insight about your views on success.

1. **What are symbols of success for you?** Are they material things or more intrinsic things? Who may have formed these ideas in your head?

2. **What is your definition of success?** Write down words that describe your idea of success and be as specific as you can.

3. **Who do you view as successful that you would not want to emulate.** Why? Has this affected decisions you have made or approaches you have taken that could be holding you back out of fear of being the same?

4. **Who do you view as successful in a positive way and would like to emulate?** Why?

5. **Has there been a major life occurrence that has shifted or evolved your idea of success and what is most important to achieve?**

EXERCISE 17:2

Now let's take a look at how your values have played into your idea of success. Pull out your Values Mind Map and compare to your answers above. When it comes right down to what makes you feel fulfilled, what values come into play and how does this translate to how you define success for yourself?

"Ask any employee of an entrepreneurial company and the one thing you will hear them say is, "I wish I could get into his/her head and understand the way he/she thinks." And herein lies the greatest source of eventual freedom from having to control every little thing to the nth degree. "

Chapter 18
Nobody Does It Better –
The Control Trap

Part of the reason that you are in business for yourself to begin with is that you felt you could do something better. We entrepreneurs take pride in this and we have every right to be proud. After all, we have built something out of nothing and most likely did it entirely our way. It's freeing and gratifying to see what we believed to have been the better way actually proven to be valid and profitable.

However, this mindset of "nobody does it better" can also cripple you to a certain extent if you take it into everything that you do. It can hamper your ability to achieve your goals if you cannot let go of all the other little things that take your time and attention away from these goals. We can control aspects of our life and work to a point of inaction, and then are not fully aware that we are the ones holding everything back.

If you have ever been accused of micromanaging, you are not alone. From the minute someone else is involved in your business, the entrepreneur tends to feel an internal pressure and concern about every task being done right — meaning, in many cases, done the way you do it. This is natural. After all, your name and personal reputation are at stake. On top of that, you have been successful because of the way you do things, so this cannot change or it could screw up what has made your business what it is. Sound familiar?

Another scenario is that you do manage to let go of control of some things and then your fear is realized. It wasn't done as you would have done it, which results in a mess to be cleaned up, a client to be appeased, a correction to be made and the confirmation that you must now be in charge of this again to see that it gets done right. If you are being honest with yourself, chances are you are also doing this in your personal life. You continue doing certain things because you think you are the only

LAY OF THE LAND

A successful landscaping company owner was faced with two frustrating realities. On the business front, the retail portion of her business was consuming her time, but not reaping profits as compared to the landscape services side of her business. On the home front, as a single parent and breadwinner, her need to take care of everything left her exhausted, irritable, and not enjoying her two children. The stress was immense and the emotional turmoil and guilt that resulted were sometimes beyond what this action-oriented business owner felt she could handle. Yet her desire to be in control of everything was what put her in this predicament.

Upon reviewing her situation on all fronts, she made a very critical business decision. She determined that the retail portion of her business was simply not profitable in comparison to the landscaping services business. And the reality was, she did not enjoy the retail side of the business, so it was a chore. In addition, the retail side was difficult to keep quality personnel who could help her run the operation, whereas she had assembled quality, loyal crews on the services side. She restructured her business around commercial and residential landscaping, sold her retail location and focused entirely on overseeing the services side of the business.

On the home front, she took a hard look at how everyone in the household could contribute to making life more enjoyable. By gaining help from her children with chores and hiring household help to supplement what they all did, she was able to get some of her life and enjoyment back. The bottom line for this entrepreneur was that she finally kept the promise, "Don't feel guilty about making life easier for yourself," and realized a more satisfying life and more profitable business.

one who can do them right, even though you really don't enjoy doing them. The need to control every aspect of your business and life is a formula for exhaustion. Does this also sound familiar?

Ask any employee of an entrepreneurial company and one thing you will hear them say is, "I wish I could get inside of his/her head and understand the way he/she thinks." And herein lies the greatest source of eventual freedom from having to control every little thing to the nth degree. Clearly no one thinks exactly the same way you think, but you can take your method for doing things out of your head and put it into an actionable procedure, system or document that will serve as a guide to others. It can also be an affirmation of your company's methods of success.

Now if you are thinking to yourself, "I don't want to do that because then it could get into someone else's hands and they could steal it and use it for themselves," you have just validated that you are a control freak. Did you hear the controlling element in that statement? Is it possible you are also concerned that someone will actually do it as well or better than you? Could your control be more about protecting your territory than growing it? If this is the case, you don't need to stagnate — just be smart. Put non-compete and confidentiality agreements into the mix so you can start moving forward again. Paranoia is no way to run your business or your life, so just put practices into place that preclude this from becoming your albatross.

How many things are you doing because you believe it will be faster if you just do it yourself rather than take the time to train someone? "Oh, I'll just do it myself." I'll bet you've said that more times than you can count, right? Think about those things that you were doing when you said this. Now, be honest with yourself. If you took the time to show someone else, how much time would that give you over the course of a day, a month or a year to concentrate on what you really should or want to be doing? Chances are it is even more than you think.

Being in charge of any given situation is not the same as having to be in control. In actuality, those who really know how to be in charge know how to delegate, create systems and processes, and gain help from others in effective ways to keep things under control without having to be in control of every aspect. Reread that statement and think about it. The best thing you can do for your sanity and to get back on track toward synergizing your life and work is to take charge of your controlling ways.

The beauty of evolving into a "take charge" mentality and out of a "being in control" mentality is that you will unleash the desire in others to take control for you. Those around you will start helping you find ways to take your company to a higher level of performance if you give them permission to take control of a particular situation.

Mind Over Matter

A second-generation owner of an international strategic consulting firm had taken her father's vision to exciting new levels with global presence and accolades. The company had evolved from being a training company to a strategic consulting business used by Fortune 100 companies around the world. The company was profitable and had doubled in size since she took the helm. However, in spite of its impressive transformation as a solutions-driven enterprise, the significant growth the owner sought was still elusive.

Part of the challenge was that several aspects of the company were still under the control of the daughter, due to limited management resources available, except in sales. Even with a staff of fourteen people, including other family members, she worked non-stop, serving as a key consultant and driver of product development in the company. In addition, she held high standards and had a great allegiance to the company's founder — her father — which made the challenge even more daunting.

Something had to give, not only for the advancement of the company, but also for her health and well being. She was continuously being pulled away from those aspects of the business she loved — product development and being the visionary of the company — because she needed to ensure that various initiatives were reaching the desired outcomes. This became especially apparent in the midst of a huge new product launch in alliance with a Fortune company client.

Attempts at placing coordinators in the roles of marketing and operations yielded less than stellar results, with still so much relying on the owner to keep the wheels turning. A long-time operational consultant had been working closely with the CEO to find the necessary funding to hire a VP of Marketing and a VP of Operations or COO, who were going to be critical to the company moving to the next level.

While outsourcing at first, the owner's strategy was to bring an entire tier of upper management into the folds of the company. Their experience and expertise would allow the CEO to confidently focus her energy where it best served the company long-term. The fact that the company was headquartered in a remote location also made attracting the right candidates challenging. After an extensive search, a terrific candidate for operations literally walked through the door as a result of this individual's family having relocated for personal reasons. The new VP of Operations was able to immediately step in and take over key operation initiatives, freeing the CEO to focus on what her passions and position dictated. In addition, the VP was able to temporarily take on the responsibility for marketing execution, which had been a critical need. The CEO very quickly felt the relief and empowerment that comes with adding the right people in the right way.

In my company, some of the best procedures we have in place came from someone other than me. These were procedures that directly advanced our way of operating in general, handling a project or serving a client. The ideas resulted because I discussed a frustration I had about a particular aspect of what we were doing and found that others in my company shared that frustration. So I asked them to come up with a solution. There is a huge amount of freedom that comes with realizing that you do not have to do all the thinking.

What if things are running smoothly at work for the most part, but in your personal life, you have this need to be in control of everything? The same principle of thinking applies here as well. Take charge versus taking control. Consider how you can get others in your life to embrace some of what you are doing to ease the constant pressure you feel to do it all. You might just be surprised how willing others are to help, especially once they see what a difference it makes in your overall demeanor and happiness.

The bottom line is that you may need to get out of your own way to see real progress begin. There is no better time than now to start taking charge.

EXERCISE 18:1

Take a look at one or more of your personal or business goals that are not making much progress at the moment. Answer these questions:

1. **What are things that you are controlling and hence, nothing is getting done?**

2. **Why, since you are controlling them, has no progress been made?**

3. **What elements are out of your control that are affecting your ability to control?**

4. **Is there something in your control personally or in your business that you wish someone else could take control of?** Do you feel like you are the only one that can do it? Why do you feel this way and is it real or imagined? Be honest. If it would be a relief to hand it off, then do it!

5. **Is there anything that you feel only you can do that could be documented or written down into a system or procedure that then could be handled by others?** Really think about this one, because this is where you can maintain control without having to be in control.

6. **What areas do you *not* want to lose control and why?** Are these valid reasons?

7. **What are some of the little incidental things that you find yourself doing because you believe it is just faster to do it yourself?** Are these things distracting you from other more important things? Are there others that could easily take these things off your plate with a little training?

"Without making attempts to go further, we may never stumble across those opportunities that open up a whole new world to us. Some of our greatest "aha" moments happen while we are striving toward something else. "

Chapter 19
Playing It Too Safe

Taking a risk is scary. Putting yourself or your business out there beyond where it was before takes guts. And with that comes the possibility that it may not go exactly as planned. But haven't you already done this when you started your business? So why are you being so cautious now?

Something happens to many business owners once they reach a certain level of comfort. It's called complacency. After working so hard and sacrificing so much, it is easy to get into a comfort zone. You feel as though you can finally take a breather and simply enjoy the fruits of your labor. Initially, this is a wonderful feeling. But let's face it, we entrepreneurs love discovery and evolution. So, after a while, we get the urge to explore new territory … and then something stops us. All of the sudden, the "what if" thinking begins to creep in and we start to analyze our motives and how a new venture could affect what we already have. That next level of growth could cause a whole new level of sacrifice that we're not convinced we really want to experience again.

For these business owners, it is their fear of taking risks that gets in the way. After overcoming many obstacles and building a successful business, a level of caution settles in, and they decide to stay in their current situation because it is safe and somewhat predictable. The problem with this approach is, over time, it becomes less rewarding. You have reached a certain level of success and yet you find yourself accepting, reluctantly, that where you are currently is okay. However, the reality is that it is not okay. You are trying to convince yourself it is because it is safer than making another attempt and potentially risking or sacrificing again.

Part of planning to succeed is taking risks. Like it or not, with each success the bar is raised. That is what achievement is about — taking whatever you desire to the next level. Part of doing this is to put plans into place and then put action into those plans. The world is filled with good intentions. But it's those who intend, and then step

HANDY MAN

When a young owner of a successful third-generation retail china and glassware boutique in France decided to sell his share of his business to his sister and move to America, most people thought he had lost it. With a family that included young children, and without any idea exactly what he was going to do, he just knew this is where he wanted to build a life and a business he could nurture from scratch. He also craved work where his love of working with his hands and his mind were challenged.

He discovered the perfect business in a pecan farm in the countryside of Georgia. Within fifteen years, he had built the farm from 861 producing trees to over 14,000 producing trees. He had achieved what he set out to do. He sold the farm and decided to semi-retire, relocating to another area of the Southeast.

He supplemented his retirement with handling investments of a select few friends who saw his own successes and wondered if he would mind managing their assets as well. While he enjoyed crunching numbers, creating complex analysis spreadsheets, and calculating shorts and covered stock options on the market, this was not where his true passions were. He missed working with his hands, realizing something tangible, and seeing the gratification that came from the end result.

Never one to be all work and no play, he always knew that there needed to be enjoyment outside of work. He was a pilot and enjoyed hiking on a regular basis at nearby national forests. He also found hobbies, such as oil painting, woodworking and baking, which allowed him to once again work with his hands. His ingenuity even inspired building a proof box humidifier for the proper preparation of crescent dough used in his baking for friends and family. He thought, "Why spend thousands of dollars, when you can make one yourself with a little sweat and resourcefulness?"

However, with all that he did to fill the void, he still wanted his work to reflect his passion of using his hands and mind to make a difference. Years earlier, he had taken a massage course. Over the years, he continued to enjoy the difference his hands could make to ease someone's pain or stress through massage.

When the economy took an unfavorable turn, he realized that he really did not want to be in the money management business any more. He also realized he had become comfortable, and also a bit more risk-averse, compared to his younger days. He determined he wanted to do something that he loved to do and that others would also appreciate. So at the age of fifty-eight he went back to school to become a neuromuscular therapist. Always a quick study and someone who puts everything into whatever he sets out to do, he not only has his vigor back, he is also viewed as a mentor to others in the profession.

forward and act, who understand that both life and business are moving targets. You must have the expectation that you will need to adapt as your plans unfold.

If you are a business owner who has already achieved a level of success, this could mean recognizing and being open to resources or activities that could help you achieve the next phase of discovery, without having to make sacrifices in the process. If you are the entrepreneur who has settled for being comfortable, this could mean discovering something that gets your juices flowing again outside of the business. All of a sudden, you may find that spark returning inside your business as well. It may spark you getting into a new line of work altogether.

There is a saying that goes, "On the way to what I planned, something better came along." Without making attempts to move forward, we may never stumble across those opportunities that open up a whole new world to us. Some of our greatest discoveries or "aha" moments happen while we are striving toward something else. This is what synergy is all about — being able to recognize the opportunity and then capitalize on it.

Entrepreneurs who have synergized their lives are discovering things about themselves and the world around them every day on both a personal and business level. You can too. It's simply a matter of stepping out of your comfort zone once again, taking some risks, and enjoying life and work in continually stimulating ways.

EXERCISE 19:1

Let's take a look at what could be holding you back so that you can unleash that entrepreneurial spirit in you once again. Answer these questions to begin to explore the possibilities:

1. **Think back to some of the biggest risks that you have taken and succeeded.** What were the elements that contributed to the success? How did you overcome any obstacles?

2. **Consider small risks that you have taken that have paid off.** Why were they small risks comparatively speaking? What made them less risky and why?

3. **What in your business, if you had to do it all over again, would you have done sooner, but the risk factor kept you from taking the plunge?** Looking back, why do you now wish you would not have hesitated? If you had not hesitated, what new result do you believe you may have realized?

4. **What risks have you taken that did not turn out as you had hoped or work out as planned?** What contributed to these results? What could you have tried or done differently? As a result of this risk not paying off, what have you determined as it relates to your business? Are you being totally honest with yourself about how it is affecting how you proceed in your business, or are you actually settling for less? Are there resources you did not tap or consider that could have helped you overcome any obstacles?

5. **What are some risks that you would like to take in your business, but are hesitant to take?** Why are you hesitant? What is the worst case scenario and what is the best case scenario? What resources could you tap to achieve this beyond your own means?

6. **What are you doing personally to challenge yourself outside of the business?** If nothing, what would you like to discover or learn that interests you?

"Thrill-seeking, can-do entrepreneurs are the most exhilarating to be around and also the most exasperating with a million and one adventures up their sleeves. Ingenious entrepreneurs are not daredevils at all, but are mavericks who are more calculated in their risks than you could possibly imagine."

Chapter 20
Being a Business Daredevil

"Tell me I cannot do something, and just watch me do it." Does this sound familiar? While this is certainly an admirable quality and very likely why you have accomplished what others may have thought could not be done, it may also be the reason you are not as far along as you would like to be in your life and in your business. Now don't get me wrong. There is a thrill to proving that you can create something that no one else has created. There is an attraction doing something that was stated could not be done. There is a validation that comes from achieving what others thought was not possible. And there are certainly profits in having a business that represents all of these things. The key is taking action with a real strategy and reason behind the bravado, and not just because someone said you couldn't.

Is there a risk that you *have not* taken? When taking a risk did not go exactly as planned, do you take time to consider all aspects of the risk and why it did not work out *or* do you simply shrug it off, dust off, and move on to the next huge opportunity without a second thought? If you have met every risk that has come your way with an adventurous spirit, then you are a daredevil that sees risk as a venture in and of itself. There is an excitement and a thrill for you in taking risks. You like to push your limits and the limits of others. You see risk as a part of who you are and without taking risks, life and business would not be rewarding or invigorating, but boring.

Being a risk-taker is a proven attribute of a successful entrepreneur. Savvy entrepreneurs know how to discern opportunities and the risks involved with a strategic eye and a calculated perspective. They also know when to pull the right mix of advisors in to analyze the risk as a means of balancing it with their own intuition and gut instinct. While not every scenario within a risk can always be anticipated, having as many of the contingencies considered helps you better adapt and respond versus being blindsided.

No Plateau in Sight

In 2001, an occupational therapist working with stroke patients grew increasingly frustrated with his industry. There was a common belief among his peers that a stroke survivor with limited function in his or her right or left arm and hand could only reach a certain plateau of recovery, and then needed to accept severe functional limitations. It was considered the norm that each patient would have to live with the fact that he or she would likely not use that arm and hand again. This expectation made the therapist's work unrewarding for him.

However, this occupational therapist became inspired by the premise of what appeared to be unconquerable. So he, along with his brother, also an occupational therapist, set out to prove the industry wrong. The first product developed was a rod with a built-in gripping splint. It allows a patient to regain control and the feeling of grasping an object while leveraging the rod in a series of repetitive exercises for strength building and endurance. The second product used a combination of plastic, padding, aluminum, springs, and connecting mechanical functionality to enhance a patient's ability to once again grasp and release.

Several patented medical devices later, and a business footprint that covers the globe, this inspired maverick and pioneer in his industry has helped thousands of patients, some twenty years post-stroke, realize the joy of using their arm and hand to do everyday tasks. Most were told that their arms or hands would never be functional again.

The key to this entrepreneur's success has been combining his "I know it can be done" attitude with a seasoned team. Together they continue to build a strong business model, gain ongoing capital investment, and realize operational stability in the midst of continuous innovation and promotion, the two areas where this entrepreneur's passion thrives.

What about those of you with ideas that come at lightning speed? Exploring a multitude of ideas on a continual basis is another daredevil trait. Some of your ideas may not even have anything to do with your current business. You simply cannot let them go, so you decide to experiment with another little venture on the side. Before you know it, you have two, three, or maybe more businesses attempting to take shape. You may even profess to be a serial entrepreneur because you have so many businesses going at one time. It sounds good. It feels good. And it also validates why you have so many "irons in the fire." The reality is, however, that you are an idea machine with no real strategy, focus or plans to back it up. You are a business owner who doesn't actually know what business you really want to be in, so you have many to keep you busy. I know this sounds harsh, but if you are really honest with yourself, you may recognize this as true. A serial entrepreneur sees businesses through to success, is able to hand them off at a certain point and *then* is able to direct focus on to the next exciting venture.

Managing numerous business ideas or even businesses can feel as though you are taking all of your talents to their greatest degree of usage. Going to the edge can be pushing the envelope to innovation and this is what can give businesses a real edge. But if you are exploring too many ideas at one time, it can also be pushing your core business into its ultimate demise because you are distracted and not giving any one venture the needed attention and nurturing.

Thrill-seeking, can-do entrepreneurs can be the most exhilarating to be around when they are focused and rallying everyone around them to strive toward the same end result. However, they can also be the most exasperating when they have a million and one ideas up their sleeves and are constantly shifting, refocusing or throwing caution to the wind — all in the spirit of being on the cutting edge. Ingenious entrepreneurs are not daredevils at all, but are mavericks who are more calculated in their risks than you could possibly imagine.

Are you ready to harness your risk-taking for truly empowered and inspired success? Then it is time to take a look at where you've been and where you are to help you become the maverick who has everyone anxious for your next great venture or idea.

EXERCISE 20:1

Do you have ideas or things that you want to do that are totally unrelated to your business, but good ideas all the same? List them and answer these questions:

1. **Is this a potential second venture for you if you had the time to pursue it?**

2. **Is this purely something for your own pleasure and enjoyment, but you just don't have the time right now to do it?** Why? Does it really take that much time? Can you free up time by reassessing your other choices to allow you this indulgence?

3. **Which ones are just cool or interesting ideas, but really have nothing to do with your business or fit into your life?** Is there someone you trust that you could share these ideas and they could take the ball and run with it?

EXERCISE 20:2

Do you have several opportunities that you'd like to take advantage of, but are not sure which ones to focus on?

1. **Why do you see these opportunities as valuable?** What does each have the potential to do for you personally or professionally?

2. **Which ones will have a direct impact on the current goals you have identified as top priorities in your business or personal life?**

3. **Which ones need to be acted upon or the opportunity may be lost?** Why? What would happen if you did not act upon them?

4. **Which ones do not require any immediate action because they will still be of value or be actionable later on?**

EXERCISE 20:3

Answer these questions to explore how being a daredevil may actually be causing you and your business to vacillate:

1. **Why do you find taking risks exciting?**

2. **What is your idea of a big risk versus a small risk?** How does this compare with others you know who take risks?

3. **What risks have you taken as a result of being told you couldn't do it or pull it off?**

4. **What risks have you taken out of boredom?**

5. **What ideas have you pursued that have nothing to do with your core business?**

6. **Do you have multiple business ideas going at once?** Are any of them moving forward and if not why?

7. **What risks paid off?** What risks did not? Can you find any common factors in why one succeeded and why others failed?

"Because it makes so much sense, because it is logical and comfortable, and most important of all, because it is proven to be doable, you, too, can put synergy in motion."

Synergy in Motion

Throughout Chapters One through Twenty, multiple real life, real business stories were shared as examples to inspire you and to help you relate, so that you too can evolve from a balanced mindset to a synergized mindset. However, some of you may still believe that this whole idea of synergy sounds great, but wonder if it can really work for you. You may want to adopt the three promises because they make sense, but are wavering in making them your own. You may relate to many of the wishful and fearful thinking limitations, yet are hesitant to progress forward.

This final section of Me, Myself & Inc. presents more than just snippets of successes. It details how real life entrepreneurs have put synergy into motion — without even realizing this is what they were doing. What came naturally to them can be adopted and practiced by you. And you will be surprised how natural it will become to you.

It really is that simple. Because it makes so much sense, because it is logical and comfortable, and most importantly, because it is proven to be doable — you, too, can put synergy in motion. The concepts in this book can become a part of how you think, empowering you to build an energized business and realize your ultimate life.

So be inspired. Be encouraged. Be synergized … once and for all.

"A week later, the home was in shambles. Priceless collectibles sold at flea markets for five dollars each, and neighbors who had lived nearby for thirty years looted the place as if the items were theirs to take."

Chapter 21
Burden Turns Golden

In her mid-twenties and enjoying a comfortable salary in a corporate job as a single professional, Julie Hall always knew she was destined for something more exceptional and unexpected. She just was not sure what that was at the time. She ventured into buying and selling antiques on the side when she found she had a natural eye for spotting items of worth in the most unexpected places. As she continued to realize success from this side venture, she still could not bring herself to leave her corporate job due to the stability and regular income it brought. Her family and friends continuously reinforced that she should not take that stability for granted.

One day, Julie was visiting the home of a 103-year-old woman who was seeking to sell her antiques and many of her possessions and then move out of her home and into an assisted living center. The woman had outlived all of her relatives, so Julie recommended the woman get some professional help to manage the overall sales process. She offered to help the woman if she was interested. The woman wanted to think about it and so Julie agreed she would stop back in a week.

Synergized Insights

Be a Pioneering Expert: Find a way to be the one to do it first or do it better. Be the voice that challenges the status quo or unacceptable practices to set a higher standard.

A week later, the home was in shambles. Priceless collectibles were taken to flea markets and sold for five dollars each, and neighbors who had lived nearby for thirty years looted the place as if the items were theirs to take. Instead of calling Julie back, the lady had mistakenly trusted long-time neighbors to help. In consoling the elderly woman, Julie realized that the woman was actually trying to console her. Julie was simply in shock by the greed and inconsiderate actions of others. Regretting not having taken Julie up on her offer, the woman said, "How I wish I would have used an estate lady like you to help me."

It was in that very moment, when Julie was twenty-seven-years of age, that The Estate Lady® property dissolution and estate liquidation business was born. Julie immediately discovered that the industry was a hunting ground by unscrupulous people eager to take advantage of the elderly. Their children and grandchildren typically did not know where to begin, so they easily trusted those in the business.

The first thing Julie set out to do was to educate, educate, educate. She vowed to help families better understand how to handle their loved one's property in the final chapters of an elderly family member's life. She was determined to be the guard dog and gatekeeper of any estate she managed for a family. At first, her age was a negative, considering that her audience was typically two to three times older than her. But she was so passionate about bringing unsavory practices to light, that she quickly earned respect, and word began to spread. She spent countless hours speaking in front of church groups to caution people about the unethical practices occurring in their own backyards. She soon became known as an advocate, building a reputation as someone who has set out to clean up the industry and its practices for the sake of families and the elderly.

Be Steadfast and True: Don't sway from your values and principles, even at the forfeiting of monetary profit. Money can always be made, but a lost reputation is harder to earn back.

Because of the way the industry had operated previously, Julie's integrity was continuously put to the test in her business. For instance: relatives wanting to pay Julie in cash so siblings would not know about her involvement; and requests for certain items to be sold "off the books" so the overall sales figures from the estate would not be reported. Each time, Julie would stand firm and true to her ethics, even at the expense of losing business. As a result of never steering from her values, she earned the strong respect of others serving estates — financial planners and estate attorneys. They repeatedly referred her, knowing the personal property within the estate would be handled with utmost professionalism and care.

Over the years, she continued to expand her own knowledge base by adding to her capabilities, including becoming a professional antiques and collectibles appraiser in addition to being a professional personal property liquidator. While business was going like gangbusters, Julie was wearing herself out. She realized she needed to add a support team to help with her business and in running the estate sales. She set high standards for those she contracted to help her with the estate sales, with a "one strike and you're out" policy. Her strictness may have appeared unreasonable, but Julie was working with clients during the most vulnerable times of their lives. Emotions ran high. Greed ran higher. And it was her job to keep everything in check and protect her clients' tangible assets.

With the help of her support team and expanded network of resources, Julie was now able to handle larger estates as well as the smaller ones. However, she also saw an opportunity to create multiple streams of income. One of her thoughts centered around the fact that a majority of her clients were baby boomers, caring for an elderly parent or relative. Having been in business now for nearly seventeen years, she had an idea for a book. While handling an estate sale for a client, she discovered the client was also a literary agent, and Julie's book idea came up in conversation. Within weeks, she was signed by the agent to a reputable, national publisher, and the pressure was on to get the book to market by June of 2008. The book's title is: *The Boomer Burden: Dealing with Your Parents' Lifetime Accumulation of Stuff.*

Initially, advisors tried to steer Julie away from her original concept that the book should be geared toward the consumer, recommending instead that the book be written as a textbook for the professional industry. However, Julie stood her ground that this book needed to be a resource for families. Her heart was with the many clients she had served over the years. She wanted her book to help as many as possible to be informed and aware, so they would not be taken advantage of or swindled out of their valuables because they simply did not know any better. To Julie, the professional could wait, but the unsuspecting consumer could not. Her tenacity prevailed and the book's original concept was pursued.

Another unique opportunity presented itself while Julie was working on the manuscript. She was approached by the owners of the American Society of Estate Liquidators,® who were interested in selling the organization. Because of Julie's high standards and reputation, she was the only one to whom they would consider selling the entity. After giving it some thought, Julie determined it would be an ideal platform to continue her mission of education and raising the standards of the

Synergized Insights

Be a Teacher: Teach as you build your business. Teach your people how to do your job and their jobs better. Teach your clients how you do business and they will reward you with more business.

Synergized
Insights

Be Resourceful:
Never approach your
business as if you are in
it all alone. Continuously
seek out and build
your business with a
collaborative mindset
that increases your circle
of influence, support
and resources.

industry. So while in the midst of the book, she also decided to update the image of the organization and prepare to launch an online training series and educational materials for the industry.

The Boomer Burden was published in June of 2008 with an overall national marketing campaign that covered the country in just a few months time. Shortly after the book's debut, Julie launched the American Society of Estate Liquidators' new website with an online course for those considering a viable home-based business, as well as online books and reference materials. Within the first six months of both initiatives being introduced, Julie's book and online products represented an additional $100,000 in income. Her dream of bringing additional streams of income beyond her consultation had come into being — and there's no end in sight, with countless opportunities to expand the product offerings.

Be Still: Take some moments every day if possible to be still. Meditate. Allow your mind to clear. Allow your spirit to rejuvenate. Even five minutes can make a big difference in your state of mind.

In reflecting on nearly twenty years in business and her next forty years of life, Julie states that she makes her decisions and is driven by a desire to not have any regrets. She says that when she is eighty-seven years old, she wants to be able to state without hesitation that she did everything she set out to do, helped others along the way, and had a rich, full life. As she takes a midday break to enjoy a facial with her twelve-year-old daughter, it is safe to say, this is indeed the way that she lives.

"Show up on time and care about the guests. Simple, but effective. Dressler's enjoys a low turnover rate with a dedicated staff in an industry where a 200 percent annual turnover is the norm.

Chapter 22
No Waiting in Line

The restaurant industry has one of the highest failure rates among small business start-ups. This may discourage some. However, for Jon Dressler and his wife Kim, a restaurant of their own was not only a dream, but a passion. The key, they knew, was to take into account all the reasons why restaurants tended to fail, and then make sure they did not make the same mistakes. Dressler's Restaurant was opened in September of 2003.

First, the Dressler's made a steadfast commitment that no one, including themselves, would work more than 40 hours-a-week. This was quite a stance to take, considering most start-up businesses within any industry usually included the owners putting in twice that amount of time per week to get the business off the ground. However, for the Dressler's, this simply was a trend they were vehemently going to defy. How did they accomplish this? By hiring enough people from the start so the responsibilities were shared among all in a manner that did not tax one person's time investment too heavily. While this was a huge financial investment, it was the only way to assure the 40-hours-or-less rule could be managed.

Synergized Insights

Be Comfortable with Mistakes: No one is perfect. Mistakes are how people learn and grow. Creating an environment where mistakes are viewed as ways to learn, versus a reason to punish, results in fewer mistakes reoccurring.

Next, Jon determined that restaurant consistency and quality food had to be a way of doing business, no matter what. If the quality of the food was never in question, this allowed the service staff to be totally focused on the guest experience. This led to the next three key things everyone needed to understand about Dressler's Restaurant. In priority order, everyone on the Dressler team knew that they should: 1) take care of the guests; 2) have fun; and 3) make money.

For the Dressler's, this was a logical sequence of order. If a guest was taken care of and everyone was having fun in the process, the staff would make money and the restaurant would make money. The Dressler's reminded staff that they were there to serve, not sell. So they were not to push the menu items, but were to know all aspects of the menu inside and out so they could answer questions and share opinions. Everyone not only knew the menu, but had tasted everything on it.

As for the rules associated with the team members, there were only two. Show up on time and care about the guests. Simple, but effective. Dressler's enjoys a low turnover rate with a dedicated staff in an industry where a 200 percent annual turnover rate is the norm. The 30 percent turnover they experience is the result of employees being fired for not adhering to the two associate rules and college students moving on to their chosen careers. Part of Dressler's success is putting senior service staff in charge of training newer staff. Jon gives his expectations speech and then the training is left in the capable hands of his experienced team.

Another set of rules Dressler's operates by is in how they approach improvements and investing in their business. When considering any change or improvement, these questions are asked in this order: Does it adversely affect the guest experience? Does it adversely affect the team morale? Does it cost money? If the answer to the first two questions are no and the answer to the last question is yes, then the investment is made. If either of the two first questions are answered with a yes, even if the change does not cost any additional money, it is not made.

They used these questions to guide their decisions when they opened a second restaurant, Max's Ally, in another part of the city. They were considering whether or not to offer lunch at the new restaurant, in addition to serving dinner. Staff from Dressler's who went there midday to get Max's Ally cleaned up and ready for the dinner crowd noticed an opportunity in the traffic that they saw at the lunch hour.

In previous years, Dressler's had considered opening for lunch, but it would have been too demanding on its people, so they stayed with dinner only. It may have been easy to discard the idea of serving lunch at Max's Ally for the same reasons, based

Synergized Insights

Be Clear with Expectations: If people know what exactly is expected of them, they will perform better and make the business better as well. Keep the expectations simple, clear and succinctly focused on what is non-negotiable and why. Too many rules can stifle ingenuity and ideas.

on what had been assessed on the Dressler's side. However, the Max's Ally area of town needed another lunch option. The employees were willing to do double-duty, so the morale was not an issue. And since the employees were already there anyway, even cost was not much of an issue. So the decision was made to offer lunch Monday through Friday, and it proved to be a profitable one.

One exception to the Dressler's rules was made when guests inquired about whether Dressler's was going to be open on Christmas Eve so out-of-town family could be entertained. The restaurant had initially determined to be closed out of consideration for its team members and their families. But guests were indicating that this could be a big money maker for the restaurant and guaranteed they would bring their families to the restaurant if it were open. Bringing it to the staff, Jon was able to get some staff members to give up their Christmas Eve with the caveat that if the restaurant did not serve at least 175 guests, they would not open Christmas Eve again. They served well over 175 guests and so they now enjoy helping their patrons impress out-of-town visitors every Christmas Eve.

Jon's philosophy of being consistent and creating an experience for guests translates into every decision he and his team make for the business. He vowed that he never wanted his restaurant to become the "in" place because he never wanted it to then become the "out" place. His focus was to bring quality food, quality service and quality ambiance together to make his restaurants places that people would make their regular destination to escape, entertain and conduct business. As a result, he quickly found that his three rules — caring for guests, having fun and making money — seemed to be the mantra of his business clientele too. Over the dinner table, business people were caring for their clients, making business deals (hence, money) and everyone certainly seemed to be having fun.

Synergized Insights

Be Open to Improvements: Give everyone the freedom to suggest how you can do business better. Then pursue what makes sense in the interest of the customer, the employees and the bottom line — in that order.

Jon also considers family an important value that cannot be overlooked in his personal life or among his staff at work. The reality is that in many cases, people spend as much, if not more, time with the people they work with as they do their own families. Jon wanted his business to feel like one big family, and he also wanted everyone to know he respected and valued the importance his staff members placed

Synergized
Insights

Be a Thinker-Doer:
Don't just think about
what you are going to
do, take action. Whether
it is to get more
information or to get
a new venture started,
just thinking about it will
get you nowhere fast.

on their families. As a regular practice before opening for the dinner crowd each evening, the chef prepares dinner for the entire wait and service staff at 4:30 p.m. During this time, current events are discussed, the newest members share a little bit about themselves, and any personal news is shared as if sitting around a family dinner table. This time has become coveted by the staff and is a key bonding experience that translates to a true caring spirit that carries over into the service in the dining room and bar.

Jon has made his business a family affair on the personal front as well. Initially starting the restaurant with his wife Kim, he has also involved his mother and children. Guests rave about the desserts his mother makes, including ordering full cheesecakes or carrot cakes at a premium price to take home. As Jon's children have grown older, they too have contributed to the ambiance that his guests enjoy. His son greets guests at the front and then pulls the chairs out for the ladies as they are seated at the table. His daughter visits guests at their tables to share conversation.

Jon has found that many assume he puts in unending hours because he is there sometimes at night when the restaurant is in full swing. Guests will comment that he must never be able to enjoy a Friday or Saturday night out. He smiles as he tells his guests that while they are working nine-to-five, he is golfing (one of his passions) or enjoying a school event with his children. And Jon adds that while his guests may have to wait in line for a table at his restaurant on Friday and Saturdays, he never has to stand in line at fine restaurants on a Wednesday or a Tuesday evening. As a matter of fact, Jon cannot recall ever having to stand in line for anything since opening his restaurant; his flexibility allows him to avoid lines while others simply have no choice.

Synergized Insights

Be Experience-Focused: The customer experience is everything to a successful business. Know what you want your customer to experience inside and out, and then create it to the finest detail.

Being consistently good at what is being done is what Jon believes has been the key to succeeding where so many others have failed. However, consistency is not accidental. It is a conscientious effort that is achieved by setting clear expectations, not sacrificing quality for the mighty dollar, and understanding who is really paying the bills — the guests.

Amidst what is considered the worse economic downturn in American history, Jon is prepared to open his third restaurant. Jon may not have to stand in lines, but he fully expects guests to be eagerly standing in line to experience his next venture.

" By 10:45 a.m. all forty-eight tee shirts were sold. A star product was born and they knew their business was officially launched. They were also scared to death by the success of the product. "

Chapter 23
Life is Good – Getting Better

How does a two-man mobile tee shirt business, with both owners traveling and living out of their vans, evolve into a $100 million business with 5,000 retailers nationwide in over twenty five countries?

The evolution of Life is good® is best described as inspired action. The company produces a unique line of comfortable apparel and accessories for men, women and children, which features playful images and positive messages.

The first inspiration and motivation for entrepreneurs (and brothers) John and Bert Jacobs was that they were artists who wanted to make a living through their art. The idea of "starving artists" did not enter their thoughts. They believed without a doubt that they would find a way or make a way — it was just not going to be the conventional way.

To make this belief a reality, they needed to be open to all resources. The idea of putting their art on tee shirts was a natural one for them. In their eyes, a tee shirt would serve as a canvas for their artwork, not a gimmick. It was a unique way to present and spread their artwork for the masses to see. It was a means of not only visually inspiring, but verbally inspiring.

Synergized Insights

Be Positive. The glass half-full mentality and focusing on what's right keeps you focused on what to do and what really matters. Negativity serves no valuable purpose in business or in life.

Another key to their success is that the Jacobs brothers envisioned a higher purpose for what they were creating, and they wanted their art to be something that anyone could own and enjoy. They began to see their mission as bringing enlightenment and empowerment to the world through their art, and it became the basis for building their business. They also believed that their products should be affordable, attainable and inclusive.

The brothers put their mission into motion selling their tee shirts at festivals on the streets of Boston and in college dormitories throughout the Northeast, slowly turning their passion into a viable business. During these lean years, an area of support that proved pivotal to success was involving friends as a quasi focus group for their concepts. Their apartment wall became a brainstorming and evolution board for messages and art. Their focus group meetings were more like parties, with friends sharing their thoughts and perspectives. Nothing formal, nothing structured, just fun. Sharing, communicating and consummating.

During two of these parties, the name Life is good® and the character Jake were born. Friends collectively helped the Jacobs brothers fine-tune hundreds of ideas into this one pivotal business-building turning point. Excited, the Jacobs' did as they always do — they took action. Within two days they printed forty-eight tee shirts for a weekend street fair that started at 10:00 a.m. on a Saturday. By 10:45 a.m. all forty-eight tee shirts were sold. A star product was born and they knew their business was officially launched. They were also scared to death by the success of the product. But this fear quickly turned into joy. They had created something that resonated with a broad demographic — from school teacher to tattooed biker, from punk rocker to all-American teen. Today, their products speak to the athlete, the skate boarder, the Baby Boomer, the environmentally conscious, the dog lover, the outdoor enthusiast, Gen X, Gen Y, the Millennium Generation, men, women and children. They had created something that spoke to the masses in a very personal and real way.

Synergized Insights

Be Authentic: Know who you are and stay true to yourself in everything you do. Live your values. Work your values. Be your values.

From that point forward, all products stemmed from the feel good, Life is good® mantra. And as the brothers built their brands and expanded their product lines, they continued to realize the power of gaining insight by hearing what others had to say. They were not afraid to make life easier for themselves. They saw the value that other minds brought to their venture and they did not get in their own way.

But after the events of September 11, 2001, there was a sense in the country and the company that life was not so good. The Jacobs called a company meeting to rally their employees and brainstorm what the company could do in response to the current state of affairs. The brothers suggested a fundraiser, but it was the employees that brought the idea to life. A suggestion was made to take an existing best-seller tee shirt displaying a stylized American flag and donate 100 percent of the proceeds to the United Way to help families affected by the tragedy. The goal was to raise $20,000 in 60 days. A total of $207,000 was raised. And all the Jacobs had to do was say yes to an idea that impassioned and energized the company to make a difference. Today the company is giving back every day with Life is good® Festivals and the Life is good® Foundation.

The company has been approached numerous times to go public or be purchased by global conglomerates. But it is the founding passion and philosophical beliefs of John and Bert Jacobs that make this not only unappealing, but unthinkable. They believe they have only begun to scratch the surface in making a difference as they continue to spread joy with their products and brands. For them, it is much more than a business. It is a way of life … and Life is good®.

Be Unwavering.
When you know you are onto something, give it all that you've got. Take charge, pull the resources together, learn as you go, and always move forward to the next opportunity.

"Preparing to go on stage for her stand-up comedy act, she knew one thing was no laughing matter — those panty lines under her white pants. So she cut off the feet of some panty hose ... and an idea was born."

Chapter 24
Thanks for Spanx®

From aspirations of being a trial attorney to working as a chipmunk at Disney World, and from selling fax and copy machines door-to-door to performing city-to-city stand-up comedy — by the tender age of twenty-seven, Sara Blakely had done it all.

Having now earned her way up the corporate ladder at the office equipment company, Sara was working as a sales trainer by day and performing stand-up comedy at night. Preparing to go on stage for her stand-up act, she knew that one thing was no laughing matter — those panty lines under her white pants. So she cut off the feet of some pantyhose ... and an idea was born. What inspired her to cut off the feet? She was wearing strappy sandals and did not want the panty hose to show, but she did want the support and smooth body lines that the pantyhose provided on top.

Talking to friends and other women, she discovered they had done the same thing to create that smooth look underneath pants. Even though she had never taken a business or marketing class, Sara knew she was onto something and she began the process of bringing her vision of a footless pantyhose product to life. On nights and weekends during the next two years, Sara focused on making a prototype, designing packaging, naming the product and securing patent protection.

After researching the hosiery manufacturing industry for months via phone calls and the Internet, Sara took a week off from work to find a manufacturer to develop her prototype. She met rejection at every turn and heard every reason why her

Synergized Insights

Be Unconventional: If your idea feels right and resonates with those you are trying to reach, don't let the fact that it has never been done that way before stop you.

product would fail, including the fact that she had no financial backing. Most thought her idea was crazy and would never sell. Fortunately, one mill owner shared Sara's idea with his daughters — and they did not think it was a crazy idea at all. The next day, the mill owner called Sara. A year later after tenacious testing of fabrics and design construction, the prototype was made.

Sara knew that, like her product, the name and packaging for her footless pantyhose had to be totally different than anything the hosiery industry had seen before. The name Spanx® was developed because it was edgy, catchy and made the mind wander. It alluded to how the product helped make a woman's butt look better, and Sara did not apologize for this brazen aspect of the product's name. The packaging also needed to attract attention. She chose illustrations and unconventional statements that would "tell it like it is." What mattered most was targeting her product for its market and she kept that idea front and center throughout the packaging design's development. She received feedback from countless women who inspired her to add this reassurance to the packaging: "Don't worry, we've got your butt covered."

Synergized Insights

Be Failure Minded: If you have a failure every day, it means you have pushed yourself beyond your comfort zone to see where it might lead. Consider failure something that you strive to experience every day so you can learn, grow, overcome, appreciate and better identify the best paths to take and decisions to make.

Getting her product to market required a national retailer. A natural salesperson, Sara had heard the word no a thousand times and did not hesitate to start right at the top, targeting major retailers that she wanted to carry her product. With tenacity and belief in her product, she called Neiman Marcus, requesting just ten minutes to show the buyer that her product was something their customers could not live without. In those ten minutes, she took the buyer into the restroom and personally demonstrated the product under her cream pants. Three weeks later, her products were on the shelves of Neiman Marcus.

With no money to advertise, Sara hit the road and personally appeared at in-store rallies to introduce the product to sales associates and customers, once again doing what no one in the hosiery industry had done before. She also used the uniqueness of the product, its risqué name and packaging, and her sense of humor to gain coverage in magazines, radio and TV. She took the initiative to send a gift basket to Oprah Winfrey, thanking the celebrity for providing the inspiration to never give up on a dream. Oprah tried the product and loved it. Before Sara knew it, she received a call that Oprah was featuring Spanx® as her product of the year. Sara continued to target celebrities to try her product — with monumental success. This resulted in endorsements from Sarah Jessica Parker, Gwen Stefani, Gwyneth Paltrow and others. Sara continues to keep her products and her approach fresh and cutting-edge for her industry. Her focus on public relations over advertising has gained her exposure in magazines like Vogue, Glamour and Forbes, as well as TV venues like Good Morning America and the Tyra Banks show.

New product development for Spanx® has always been motivated from a clear purpose — to promote comfort and confidence for women. Sara and her team are in continuous communication with the end customer to discover their needs, in order to develop solutions that offer women comfort in what they wear and confidence in how they feel. Since the first prototype, more than 100 styles have been developed, including an entirely new product line called Assets.

Even before starting her company, Sara had a goal of helping women who do not have the same rights as women in America. This fit perfectly with her company's mission of helping women realize greater comfort and confidence in their lives. The Sara Blakely Foundation made this dream a reality, established with $750,000, to help women globally through education and entrepreneurship. A percentage of every product's sales goes toward the Foundation.

Six years after launching Spanx® in her apartment, with only $5,000 and a blind, unwavering faith, Sara is recognized as the pioneer of a $150 million global enterprise and an inspiration to women around the world.

Synergized Insights

Be Confident, Not Ignorant: Know what you are good at doing, and then hire the right people to do what you are not good at. Don't let your lack of knowledge hold you or your company back. Once you accept this, you can operate from a place of total confidence.

"The next challenge came when Janet received a call from a competitor's law office with a cease and desist directive. This took Kirk and Janet by surprise, and they knew it could mean a significant financial drain to the company if they could no longer market the product.

Chapter 25
One Big Family

From the time Kirk and Janet were married in 1971, they understood that looking at their personal and professional goals was a dynamic way to view their future. She was a CPA and he was a banker. Once they had children, she started practicing accounting part-time. He left his banking position and along with a business partner, formed a corporation that sold banking equipment. Janet got involved on the accounting side, setting up the books and managing entries.

The business proved lucrative and they were living the high life. Their children were in private school and they had all the material luxuries. But in spite of this, after a few years, Kirk was no longer enjoying the business. It was monetarily satisfying, but not something he was passionate about. In addition, he and his partner did not agree on how the company should grow and be managed. As tensions mounted, Kirk and Janet determined it would be best for the partner to buy out their portion of the business. Kirk was back on the market again.

Synergized
Insights

Be Agile:
Opportunities often come where and when you least expect them. Being alert and aware enables you to see what others may miss.

He had a friend who sold wheelchairs made by a German company and Kirk was intrigued by the product. He investigated further and was soon hired as national sales manager for the company. During a trip to Europe, Kirk and the same friend learned of a Scotland-based company called Snug Seat that was looking for a distributor in the U.S. and Canada. The company specialized in equipment for children with physical disabilities. The two men discussed with their wives the idea of becoming a U.S. distributor. Kirk's friend's wife taught children with disabilities. The two couples decided to set up a corporation. The women would run the operation and the men would provide operational support as needed, while maintaining their day jobs. Neither couple had discretionary funds to invest in the business, so the company was set up with very little capital.

The U.S. distributor arm of Snug Seat was established in 1987, importing products from Snug Seat in Scotland. Their first challenge came when the child car seat did not pass U.S. crash test standards. With considerable outside help, they were able to redesign, manufacture, and successfully bring a new version to market within ninety days. Additional equity was required to solve the redesign and manufacturing issues, so the couples brought in ten new investors, but still maintained controlling interest.

Synergized Insights

Be Diplomatic.
Regardless of the challenge, try to find the win-win. Consider the other side, and then operate from a position of collaboration and respect. Being able to shift perspectives can make the difference between a good resolution and a great one.

The next challenge came when Janet received a call from a law office with a cease and desist directive. The Snug Seat was infringing on a patent of this company, despite assurances from the UK Snug Seat company that they had the right to authorize a remanufacturing agreement. This took Kirk and Janet by surprise, and they knew it could mean a significant financial drain to the company if they could no longer market the product. Kirk decided to meet with the managing director of the company and speak from the perspective of the market they served — the children. The end result was that they could continue manufacturing the product if they paid a four percent royalty. The catch was that the royalties had to be paid retroactively, from the time that the product first hit the market. This represented a cost of over $50,000.

Being a small company, this was a serious sum of money. Kirk, Janet and their partners needed to find a way to raise this money and keep their business going. They determined that they would invite their industry suppliers, manufacturers and sales reps to become shareholders in the company. Within days, they had raised the money needed and had twenty-four shareholders with interests in the company.

Kirk's friend and business partner later joined the company full-time as a manager. However, the business soon started losing money and discontented shareholders saw their investment losing its value. A change was needed to keep the company from going into bankruptcy.

The shareholders determined that Kirk needed to manage the company full-time. He left his position as general manager of the German company's U.S.

operations, immediately cutting the family's household income in half. Stressed financially, Kirk and Janet took measures to simplify their lifestyle. They shared one car, eliminated all luxuries and took their children out of private school. The company — the financial lifeblood for their family — was in a turnaround mode.

Six months later their original partners resigned from the company. The board became stronger and took a more active role in setting strategy for the organization. Although still on shaky financial ground, Snug Seat began to make progress by controlling expenses and expanding markets. Several new products were successfully introduced, and the couple's household income increased. By the end of a year, they rewarded themselves with a second vehicle — a minivan.

Kirk had been nurturing a business relationship with the representative of a line of Danish products that were a perfect compliment to Snug Seat's existing line. In 1993, Kirk met the Danish company's owners, and learned they already had a distributor out of Sweden marketing in the U.S. The distributor was not performing to their satisfaction, but it was two years before Kirk could persuade them to make the switch to his company. Finally, in 1995, Snug Seat added the Danish product line. Sales started booming. Janet was now operating as the financial controller for the company and profits soared.

By 1997, the Danish products company, R82, was interested in establishing a subsidiary in the U.S. to market its products, and asked Kirk to leave Snug Seat to help form the subsidiary. Instead, Kirk convinced R82 to buy out the other shareholders and to continue expanding and growing Snug Seat. The deal was struck, and twenty-two shareholders were ecstatic at the return on their investment. Many stayed on as part of an industry advisory board.

The company had now grown to forty-two employees. What is especially impressive about this company and the way that Kirk and Janet have managed it is the loyalty they have earned with their employees. Ask any employee about the couple and you would think they were talking about two family members, not their bosses. Likewise, Kirk and Janet consider their employees to be an extension of their family. Many have been with them since the company first hired employees. In addition, two left with the couple's blessing and encouragement for another opportunity and then came back because it "just was not the same." At a time when most employees

Synergized
Insights

Be Considerate:
Treating others with the same compassion, consideration and appreciation that you desire brings loyalty, ingenuity and fierce support in return.

remain with a company for three to five years at best, Kirk and Janet have found that once hired, their employees stay on and are impassioned about the business.

The secret to this company's success is a management team that does not micromanage, but allows employees to do the job they were hired to do. Hiring right in the first place is key. Kirk and Janet believe that it has to be a combination of skills and attitude — with attitude having the edge. They hire employees who are proactive on behalf of the business and who don't get so caught up in their job descriptions that they fail to grow within the company.

In addition, Kirk and Janet understand that in order for employees to do their job effectively, all processes, procedures and systems need to be in place. As Janet realized the need to hand off various aspects of accounting such as payables, receivables and shipping processing, she set up the associated systems and procedures for the newly hired employee. Both Kirk and Janet have always been open to suggestions and improvements from employees, resulting in greater efficiencies and better ways of doing things.

Synergized Insights

Be Strategic & Responsible:
Conduct an annual audit of your books and revisit your business plan every two to three years. Show how you are being fiscally responsible from a shareholder's perspective. This is true even when you are the only shareholders.

Another key to keeping good, dedicated employees is respecting that they have a life outside of the business. Kirk and Janet look at the company benefits from an employee's point of view. They offer a matching 401(k) plan, automatic vacation days, half-day Fridays, additional paid holidays, incentive trips and monthly employee lunches. Kirk and Janet believe a happy employee begins with a satisfied, fulfilled life.

Employees share the owner's conviction that the company is not just selling equipment, but it is operating for the greater good of the market it serves It is helping children with disabilities lead better lives. The equipment and products sold are just a means to that end. This belief feeds a level of customer service, support, innovation and problem-solving in the Snug Seat team that has customers raving. In addition, the company has adopted Easter Seals as its charitable cause, and Kirk sits on the board of the local Easter Seals/United Cerebral Palsy Advisory Board.

Janet retired in 2004, and another controller was brought in. As a shareholder, Janet still stays involved and Kirk still considers her a key contributor to the company's success. What makes this couple an extraordinary example to other husband-wife entrepreneurs is their savvy in knowing what worked best for them from the beginning. Because they looked at their life and work as one big picture, they could set guidelines for living and working together that made even the tough times easier. Rule number one was when they left the office, the family and children were the priority. No discussions of business around the dinner table or at Sunday brunch.

Another steadfast rule was a clear division of responsibilities in the company, but not on the home front. If a child became sick during the day, whoever had the most pressing demands at work would stay and the other would tend to the child. Household chores were generally viewed as a team effort.

Being of service to one another seemed a natural part of their partnership in life and in business. When one of them felt overwhelmed, the other never hesitated to step in and help. This also extended to their relationship with their employees. If shipping needs a hand, Kirk just rolls up his sleeves to assist. If an employee has a personal issue, the company flexes to allow the employee to handle it without on-the-job pressure.

Snug Seat has been in business now for almost twenty-two years. The company is realizing its most profitable year to date and experiencing record sales months, in spite of a down economy. But the bottom line for the company is that it is one big happy family — its members love what they do, see the difference they are making, and reap both emotional satisfaction and financial rewards.

Be a Philanthropist: You are not remembered for the dollars that you have made, but for the people and causes you have helped.

"Countless scoops and 27,102 pounds later, they had built the largest ice cream sundae the state had ever seen. Before they knew it, word had spread across the state. They knew the time was right for them to begin to market up and down the east coast."

Chapter 26
Sweet Taste of Success

When Jerry Greenfield and Ben Cohen, two childhood friends born four days apart, decided to start a food business, it wasn't something they had ever thought about as kids. After high school, one pursued a career in medicine. The other tried various stints at college and then dropped out to teach pottery. While one worked as an ice cream scooper in the college's cafeteria, the other dabbled in ice cream-making while helping students with their pottery making. They kept in touch and shared an apartment for a short time as they explored their individual interests.

Jerry had received yet another medical school rejection. Ben had worked as everything from a taxi cab driver to a night-shift pediatric room clerk. When they united to share an apartment together for a second time, Jerry was working as a lab technician in New York. They decided to go into the food business together. At first, they considered making bagels, but the necessary equipment was too expensive. So instead, they decided to make ice cream, thinking it would be a viable business. They paid five dollars to take a local course on ice cream making and began looking for a town that did not have an ice cream parlor. In 1978, Ben and Jerry discovered that Burlington, Vermont needed an ice cream scoop shop. They invested $12,000 of their own money, along with a $4,000 loan, to open their first store in a converted gas station.

Synergized Insights

Be Fun & Festive: Bring laughter, humor, and celebration into your business. Others will enjoy it and want to do business with you as a result.

From the beginning, they knew their homemade ice cream parlor was going to be like no other. Jerry had a passion for putting together unique combinations of flavors. He made all the ice cream for the shop, and without test marketing, created some of the parlor's first memorable flavors. Ben was the taste-tester, co-scooper and marketer of the business, devising creative ways to get the community's attention and attract people into the shop.

From the beginning, Ben & Jerry's embraced the community by making their shop a place people wanted to visit beyond just sampling the ice cream. From the onset, they shared their commitment to recycling, water and energy conservation, and the use of all natural ingredients and processes. They became known for their movie-fests, projecting movies on the wall of their building. People who came out of curiosity always stayed awhile to enjoy some ice cream. Ben and Jerry's festive approach to everything — from flavor combinations to ice cream names — quickly made a name for their business.

Synergized Insights

Be Giving & Appreciative:

Understand the power of giving without expecting anything in return. Realize the reward that comes from consistently making a difference and showing your appreciation in the smallest of ways.

On their one-year anniversary, as a way of saying thank you to the community that supported their first year's success, Ben & Jerry's offered a free single scoop of ice cream to anyone who walked in the store. This tradition still is practiced today in every Ben & Jerry's shop, with people lined up for blocks to enjoy the free treat.

Always seeking ways to expand and grab attention, the two founders decided to sell their unique ice cream flavors in pint-sized containers in grocery stores. By 1980, they were selling to grocery chains within the state of Vermont. Never shy, they decided to go for the state record. Countless scoops and 27,102 pounds later, they built the largest ice cream sundae the state had ever seen. Before they knew it, word had spread across the state. They knew the time was right for them to begin to market up and down the east coast.

During the 1980s, they introduced signature flavors such as New York Super Fudge Crunch and Cherry Garcia. In 1983, they opened their first shop outside of Vermont — in Maine. By 1987, sales were up to $32 million. Their innovative flavors and attention-getting events gained exposure on many fronts. After the stock market crash in 1987, they offered free scoops of their flavor, Economic Crunch, on Wall Street. Before long their ice cream parlors were operating in eighteen states, and in 1988, President Ronald Reagan named them the U.S. Small Business Persons of the Year.

Riding a solid wave of growth through the mid-1980s, the company met monumental challenges when their expansion resulted in a lawsuit for distribution rights against a competitor brand. Ben and Jerry quickly realized that they needed to hire someone with business acumen to steward the company's future growth and protect its mission and assets. The company's brand had been built on the unique personalities and values of its founders, Ben and Jerry. Fortunately, the new leadership provided sound business strategies, while maintaining the company's quirky culture and appeal.

Ben & Jerry's made its mark because of the wacky combinations and chunky mix-ins to its flavors, but research showed the most popular ice cream flavor in America was still plain vanilla. To meet this challenge, the new leadership introduced a line of "Smooth, No Chunks!" to satisfy that segment of the market.

The Ben & Jerry's Foundation was founded in 1985 to offer competitive grants to not-for-profit grassroots organizations dedicated to facilitating progressive change by addressing the root causes of societal or environmental problems. The foundation was established to support the company's founding values of environmental respect and social and economic justice. The company contributes a minimum of $1.1 million annually to the Ben & Jerry's Foundation, employee community action programs and corporate grants.

Unilever was impressed with the philanthropy and innovations inspired by Ben and Jerry, as well as the company's strong strategic leadership. In 2000, the international food giant purchased the ice cream company for $326 million. Unilever continued to market Ben & Jerry's separately from the company's other ice cream brands because of its memorable brand, image and culture.

Jerry now focuses his attention on his other passion — social and environmental initiatives — and serves as the president of the Ben & Jerry's Foundation. Ben is on numerous boards, is actively involved in promoting socially responsible business practices and is in great demand as a speaker.

Synergized Insights

Be Socially Conscious: Do whatever you can within your business to make the world a better place to live. Make it an integral way you do business that inspires others to do the same in their life and their work.

"The company went above and beyond to be more than just a place to work for its employees including offering $100 bonuses for every six months of continuous employment, home computer-purchase programs and first-time homebuyer assistance programs."

Chapter 27
Paper Trails – Customers for Life

In 1991, when A.J. Wasserstein, at age twenty-four, decided to start a records storage company, the reaction by most was: "What a boring business." While archiving files for customers was not the most glamorous business venture, Wasserstein knew his newly hatched business had an exciting future ahead. Why? Because he had done his homework.

In business school, Wasserstein had done extensive research on numerous business opportunities. Many opportunities were more exciting, but none had the foundational elements for a truly sustainable business like records storage. He liked the fact that once you acquire a customer, you have a customer for life — the company becomes an extension of that customer because of storing its records. He also liked that cash flow could be easily projected and calculated due to the steady billing nature of the business. Family and friends invested $70,000 to enable Wasserstein to buy a brick building for the business and ArchivesOne was born.

ArchivesOne's target customers were law firms, healthcare practices, large corporations and insurance companies. Even though his business was focused on the storage of records, he knew it was really about relationships. Because of the sensitive nature of the records his company would be responsible for, making relationships the core of every business decision was key to building trust and loyalty. From the beginning, Wasserstein focused on the fact that his business kept customers for life. He knew this required good people within his company. He also knew that a business is as

Synergized Insights

Be Leading Edge: Technology can be one of your greatest customer service advantages when put to use properly. It makes serving your customer effortless so you can focus on continually creating more value in the customer relationship.

exciting as the entrepreneur makes it. The enthusiasm for any new business venture begins with the entrepreneur's emotional investment — and it can be contagious.

Therefore part of turning his "boring" business into something exciting was to take a creative approach to customer and employee relations. Making the company fun to do business with and fun to work for was critical. This began with how he viewed his own role in the company. Wasserstein preferred the title, Director of Customer Happiness, over the boring title of President. By leading the charge to always focus on the customer, he was also leading a team that was always focusing on the customer.

Synergized Insights

Be Scientific: Do your research even before deciding what business you are going to be in. Every business has its own economic characteristics. Choose a business that will prove to be a solid business model for the long term.

Exceptional service was at the heart of what keeping customers happy was all about. To objectively evaluate the quality of their customer service on an ongoing basis, the company surveyed both clients and employees every six months. The survey gave management a qualitative and quantitative gauge on how they were performing for their internal clients (their employees) and their external clients (their customers). The company put top priority on keeping their employees happy. Wasserstein knew that speedy, courteous service was a reflection of a satisfied workplace. Happy employees meant happy customers.

Because the labor market was tight at the time the company was getting off the ground, Wasserstein knew it was extremely important to have benefits programs in place. He looked for creative ways to attract, retain and develop good employees. He wanted to keep them motivated, stimulated and most important of all — happy. Investing in his employees was as important as investing in his operations and customers. The company went above and beyond to be more than just a place to work for its employees including offering $100 bonuses for every six months of continuous employment, home computer-purchase programs and first-time homebuyer assistance programs.

By 2000, the company had grown from a local records storage company in Connecticut with a handful of employees to a company 60+ people strong, serving more than 1000 businesses in Connecticut, Massachusetts and New Jersey. A year later, the company was 90+ people strong , with 1500 customers with eight document storage warehouses. By 2003, the company was 3000+ customers strong and Inc.

Magazine named the company on its national list of the five fastest growing private companies.

ArchivesOne's fast growth and customer service was managed with the help of technology. Having numerous sophisticated support systems in place ensured nothing was left to chance when it came to a customer's files or an employee's ability to do their job. Technology served a pivotal role in enhancing sales, customer service and operational efficiencies. An online customer relationship management (CRM) and lead-tracking system was put into place to support the sales and customer service team. Package delivery software with bar-coding at point of receipt, similar to the UPS process of recording and tracking, was used. Web-based software was implemented to facilitate records retrieval. Fire suppression and security technology was structured into every storage facility for the protection and safe-keeping of the records. And employees use sophisticated hand-held scanners with printers that can print an on-the-spot receipt during delivery runs.

While technology was used to better serve customers, being smart about the technology proved to be good for the company's bottom line and image as well. The company's ability to document that it doubled its productivity over a four-year period as a result of technology initiatives earned ArchivesOne the Malcolm Baldrige National Quality Award.

By 2007, ArchivesOne had grown to be the third largest records management company in the United States with over 400 employees, 10,000 customers and sales exceeding $50 million. Its growth could be attributed to strong business practices and more than thirty acquisitions since its start in 1991. In May of 2007, the company was purchased by Iron Mountain, which yielded a 41 percent return to investors.

In spite of its meteoric growth, the company's management never lost sight of its founder's focus on nurturing relationships, internally and externally. Training Magazine ranked ArchivesOne in the top 125 organizations in the field of employee development in 2007. For Wasserstein, taking care of employees meant they would take care of the customer. And good customer service is simply good business.

Synergized Insights

Be About the Relationship:

Never let any relationship inside or outside your company go stale or unaddressed. Everything in business is accomplished with the help of other people. Focusing on nurturing and supporting relationships will ensure a well nurtured business.

ArchivesOne is a trademark of Iron Mountain Incorporated.

"There is no more powerful way to keep synergy flowing than to remember the three promises. Make these a part of everything you do every day … and with every challenge."

Conclusion
Work/Life Synergy
The Time is Now

Benjamin Franklin discovered this the hard way.
Oprah Winfrey knew this from the time she was a child.
Bill Gates now dedicates billions knowing this is key.
Tiger Woods has never lost sight of this.

A nd the thirty-five entrepreneurs presented in this book also know this to be true and life-transforming. By now, I hope that you too, have transformed your thinking to work/life synergy in achieving your goals. You are now given permission to admit and accept that work/life balance does not work and never has. It's time to let go of that "balancing" mindset that feeds guilt, sacrifice, frustration, inaction and a continuous focus on fixing what is out of balance.

You now know that you have been focusing on the wrong equation. It was not about adding things up to make them equal. It is about bringing them together to make them even more. Instead of trying to balance work/life, you need to bring together all aspects of your work/life and make them work in unison instead of against one another.

Like the entrepreneurs we admire and those cited in this book, you can start incorporating these principles into your life/work plan and see amazing things start to happen. You too can create a synergized world ... an energized business ... and the ability to live your ultimate life.

What's Next?

Chances are that as you were reading this book, you took part in some of the exercises at the end of each chapter, but moved on to other chapters without doing the exercises. I know how entrepreneurs operate — I did not really expect you to complete every single exercise in this book. Use the sections noted on page 200 to guide you through the process. But first, read this final synergized example to inspire you even more on the next two pages.

InSiteful Vision

Chuck Boyle was burned out. He had a fast-growing soil testing and construction monitoring engineering firm, but he was living a life of all work and no play. As a licensed pilot, he dreamed of having more time to fly. Chuck also wanted to enjoy his hobby of photography, but how and when? His days were consumed with his business.

One day he was flying with a friend, who was also a pilot. He realized how much he had been missing the freedom that came with being up in the sky. As they flew, Chuck pointed out various housing and business developments his firm was responsible for to his friend. That's when a new idea clicked for him. He suddenly saw these properties in a different way.

Chuck remembered his army reconnaissance training, which taught him skillful observation of the land and its surroundings. He began to take mental aerial snapshots, imagining what kind of photographs he could take if he combined his technical and reconnaissance expertise. He thought about what would happen if he incorporated technology to create imagery that not only depicted what was seen from the sky, but what was not seen by the untrained eye.

Inspired by his vision, Chuck explored the idea further. He sought out advisers and soon realized he was onto something that was not being done. Within eighteen months, he created a new division in his company called InSiteful Imagery.® Within one more year, Chuck was training aerial photographers around the country to enhance their services through this engineering technology. The Professional Aerial Photographers Association recognized him as an industry innovator and pioneer.

When the economy took a turn for the worse in 2008, Chuck fully realized the value of his new division. While his competitors were feeling the pain, and other aspects of his engineering firm were suffering due to stalled construction projects, his new division kept his business busy and sales coming in. Chuck secured government and private industry contracts and he continued to train others in this new visual technology. In December of 2008, InSiteful Imagery services skyrocketed from comprising 10 percent of his company's sales to 50 percent of its sales.

Inspired by his two personal goals to fly and to take photographs again, Chuck created an entirely new division for his company. He now has a company plane. He also has the support and resources to run his company and enjoy life more. When he is not flying and overseeing the Insiteful Imagery aspect of the business, he is spending time with family, flying for pleasure or taking photos for the sheer joy of it. And it all started with a dream and a wish.

InSiteful Imagery is a registered trademark of Chuck Boyle.

Gaining Synergy

Now that you have finished reading the book, if you have not done so already, go back and be sure to complete the exercise in Chapter Seven. Determining where your mindset is in relation to your business and personal life is an important first step in your journey toward synergy. Then, complete your Goals Mind Map (Chapter One) and your Values Mind Map (Chapter Eight). You must have these three pieces as the basis to truly begin.

After capturing your goals and values on your Mind Maps, focus on the remainder of the exercises in Chapter Eight to begin to define your personal and business mission. Then look at your Mind Maps as a whole as you return to the exercises in Chapter Three (to eliminate goals that are not yours and never were) and in Chapter Nine (to see your goals as a universe designed to help all areas of your life).

Putting Synergy into Motion

In Section Two, you may have read some wishful or fearful thinking factors that were personally familiar to you. It is now time to overcome these thought barriers once and for all. Go back to the chapters that resonated with you. Complete the appropriate exercises to begin to overcome your wishful thinking, conquer your fears and make your goals a reality.

Keeping Synergy Flowing

There is no more powerful way to keep synergy flowing than to remember the three promises. Make them to yourself each day with every opportunity and challenge that comes before you.

1. I will find a way or make a way.
2. I will not feel guilty about making life easier for myself.
3. I will be open to all possible resources and support.

Make these a part of everything you do so you can keep synergy flowing. It really is that simple … so let the synergy begin!

Acknowledgements

The following companies and entrepreneurs inspired stories or were instrumental in securing stories to share in Chapters 1 through 20:

Artist's Eye Photography, Wesley Stearns

Blueline Computer, LLC, Chris Steele

Boyle Consulting Engineers, PLLC, Chuck Boyle

Clickcom, Inc., John Dicristo, Nick Dicristo, Jon Szymanski

Cooking Uptown, Karen Cooley

CornerStone United, Inc., Tom Garlow, Bill Garlow

Delta V Forensic Engineering, Inc., Brian K. Anders

(ec)2 llc, Terry Ainsworth

Epro, Inc.

G-Force International, Inc., Gina Columna

Hearn Wealth Management, LLC, John W. Hearn III, CPA, CFP®

Heather Cook Skelton, Attorney at Law

JHE Productions, Inc., Jay Howard

Kaleidoscope Business Options, Inc., Mary Bruce

Lanier Media, Inc., Guy Maher

Laurel Wealth Advisors, LLC, John W. Hearn III, CPA, CFP®

Marcel Fromond, Neuro-Massage Therapist

Monaghan Group PLLC, Beth Monaghan CPA

Money Counts, Inc., Debbie Peterson

OIA Global Logistics, Junki Yoshida

Paradise Gardens, Marta Carlson

Pippin Home Designs, Inc., Jennifer Pippin AIBD, CPBD

Premier Resources, Angela Mastoras Key

Premier Healthcare Resources, Angela Mastoras Key

Project Live Green, Jennifer Pippin AIBD, CPBD

Queen Associates inc, QAi3, Frances Queen

Rahe Lynne Clothier, Inc. Lynne Bird

Saebo, Inc., Henry Hoffman, MS, OTR/L

SPARK Publications, Inc., Fabi Preslar

Sēk, Wesley Stearns

Index

In Appreciation

Special thanks to the following individuals who have been my greatest supporters, friends, confidantes, and cheerleaders. They are valued in my life, my business, and through various stages in the creation of this book.

Terry Ainsworth
Patsy Black
Kelly Borth
Maggi Braun
Mary Bruce
Pat Coffey
Gina Columna
Cindra and Steven Cowen
Mary Ellen Ezarsky
Julie Hall
Sandie Hawkins
Marcia Jackson
Wayne Kelly
Jan King
Ann Lampron
George McAllister
Amanda Merchant
Elizabeth Miller
Dean Palmer
Ben Palmer
Debbie Peterson
Jenny Pippin
Rosemarie Printz
Brad Rivers
Steven Scribner
Monica Smiley
Kristina Smith
Tamara Strupp
Janet Sumney
Bonnie Sweeting
Dave Yochum

About the Illustrator

Gary Palmer has been a freelance illustrator for over 30 years. A 1978 graduate of Ringling School of Art in Sarasota, FL, Palmer now works from his home studio in Charlotte, NC. His versatility in both style and art mediums has made him a much sought after illustrator to regional and national advertising agencies, corporations, institutions, magazine and book publishers. His works have been recognized with numerous awards from the Advertising Federation (Addy) and the New York Art Director's Show as well as being featured as among the best of the best in Communication Arts and Print magazines.

About the Author

Sherré DeMao is passionate about helping entrepreneurs prosper in life and in business, and has dedicated her twenty-five-year career to this purpose. Sherré is founder and Chief Marketeer of SLD Unlimited Marketing/PR, Inc., a full-service marketing consulting and strategy firm she established in 1984. Sherré helps owners of start-up and small to medium-sized companies become more savvy managers and marketers by providing innovative operational and marketing guidance, solutions and services.

Her firm's creative solutions have won numerous awards including Telly, ProAd, PICA, Addy and IABC Crown awards. Her entrepreneurial savvy and dedication to small business has earned her local, regional and national recognition. In 2004, she was honored with a National Leadership Award for her small business advocacy. As a result of chairing a National Procurement Task Force, Sherré co-authored a white paper on federal government contracting practices with small, women-owned and minority-owned business. Published by the National Association of Women Business Owners in February 2006, the paper included 34 recommendations to federal agencies, which were presented to subcommittees relevant to procurement agenda on Capitol Hill. The white paper is still being used as a resource today. These efforts were among the reasons she was recognized in 2006 as a Small Business Woman Champion by the Small Business Administration. In 2007, Sherré was named among the 50 Most Enterprising Women in North America by Enterprising Women Magazine.

As an entrepreneurial business expert, Sherré frequently provides commentary and perspective to local and national media. She writes the monthly Savvy Business Owner column in Northeast Business Today and is a contributing writer to Enterprising Women Magazine, inspiring more than 200,000 business owners online and in print.

Sherre' puts her unique philosophy and insights into practice, living a synergized life with her three daughters and a wonderful group of extended family and friends.

Printed in the United States
154280LV00003B/2/P